# WOMAN PRAYER
# WOMAN SONG

## OTHER PUBLICATIONS
## BY THE AUTHOR

### Books

Preparing the Way of the Lord
God-With-Us: Resources for Prayer and Praise
Why Sing? Toward a Theology of Catholic Church Music
An Anthology of Scripture Songs

### Records/Cassettes/Published Music Collections

Joy Is Like the Rain
I Know the Secret
Knock, Knock
Seasons
Gold, Incense, and Myrrh
In Love
Sandstone
Remember Me
Mass of a Pilgrim People
RSVP: Let Us Pray
Songs of Promise
WomanSong

# RESOURCES FOR RITUAL

# WOMAN PRAYER
# WOMAN SONG

## MIRIAM THERESE WINTER

**Illustrated by
Meinrad Craighead**

MEYER
STONE
BOOKS

Permission to make copies of a ritual in whole or in part for one-time private use for the sole purpose of facilitating community prayer is hereby granted, provided that such copies are colllected after use and destroyed. This permission does not extend to the reproduction of the songs outside the context of these rituals.

Medical Mission Sisters, copyright owners and administrators of the songs in *WomanPrayer, WomanSong,* grant permission for one-time use of the songs in noncommercial community prayer settings. Written permission must be obtained to include a reproduction of any of these songs in a nonprofit community songbook or in any publication for sale, or to use these songs in any gathering where a paid registration is required.

**Also Available:**

*WomanSong* (the songs from *WomanPrayer, WomanSong*)

• Double Cassette Album
• Melody/Text Songbook (for group singing)
• Piano Accompaniment Edition (with vocal harmonies)

Available from Meyer • Stone, at your local bookstore, music store or directly from: Medical Mission Sisters, 77 Sherman Street, Hartford, CT 06105.
Please use the Hartford address for information and permissions pertaining to all songs by the Medical Mission Sisters.

Illustration by Meinrad Craighead

Cover and text design by Evans-Smith & Skubic, Inc.

Published by Meyer • Stone Books,
a division of Meyer, Stone, and Company, Inc.,
714 South Humphrey, Oak Park, IL 60304

Manufactured in the United States of America.
92  91  90  89  88        5  4  3

Meyer • Stone ISBN 0-940989-00-X

Photo Identification page 4:
Miriam Therese Winter in Ethiopia,
at an intensive feeding center
which she helped establish in 1985.

# CONTENTS

# PREFACE

I spent the summer of 1985 in Ethiopia, where I came face to face with the devastating truth of human hunger and was an eyewitness, more than once, to the cold, hard fact of death by starvation. The images and the reality of that experience are at the heart of the creative impulse that gave birth to *WomanPrayer, WomanSong*.

Women of Ethiopia, my sisters, I am haunted by my memories of you, for you are to me every woman, and your deprivation is every woman's pain. When I had to turn you away with no kilo of grain and no cup of oil because I had none to give, I felt the emptiness and the hunger of all women everywhere who hover on the edge of survival, who lack life's basic necessities, who are deprived of opportunity, of fundamental human rights. When I saw you bent beneath staggering loads of wood or straw strapped to your back, yoked in spirit to those beasts of burden, similarly laden, plodding along at your side, I was filled with rage at the intolerable burdens so many women carry and the indignities they are forced to endure. When I sat in your woman circle, shoulder to shoulder, while the monsoon rain ran rivers of mud along the walls of our grass-roof hut, I was pierced to the heart with your wail of agony as you closed your baby's eyes in death, and I heard our Mother God howl in pain at your pain, felt Her cradle your child, Her child, close to Her maternal heart. Your tears when I left you were the tears of every inevitable separation, the letting go of every unrealized expectation, the relinquishing of promises and dreams. Thank you for the songs you sang in the midst of so much suffering, and thank you for the dancing. You affirm what I have known all along, that ritual is central to our soul's survival, that women are the celebrants of the mystery of life. The ability to find joy in the midst of sorrow and hope at the edge of despair is woman's witness to courage and her gift of new life to all.

Women of the world—of the First World, Fourth World, of the North and of the South, women of poverty and of privilege, of every culture and every color, of every country and every clan—we are, all of us, sisters. We stand together in the face of injustice. We stand together in solidarity. We stand for integrity for all people. We will make every effort to overcome whatever would divide us, the exclusion perpetuated by religious and social systems, the hierarchy of position and the priority of gender, the oppressive distinctions of caste or class. .

*WomanPrayer, WomanSong* speaks to these concerns, not through a thematic ritualization of issues, but at a more fundamental level, the level of those unaddressed assumptions that shape our beliefs and influence our actions. Indeed, the injustice I have witnessed and continue to experience is perpetuated by a systemic exclusion of the feminine from power and consequently from an opportunity to make a difference in those areas where it really counts — not only in political and economic contexts but also, and especially, in religion. It is in religion—and precisely in religious ritual—that we must make room for the unique contributions of women, so that all of God's people, women and men, might have a more balanced understanding of our common humanity and a more holistic appreciation of the gift of life.

In Christianity, the status of women is the consequence of a worldview shaped by centuries of ritual behavior that rehearses and continually reaffirms that women are subservient and therefore excluded by the rules from certain roles. This devaluation of women is theologically supported and ritually justified by the prevailing conviction that the God of Christianity is male. What a tragic loss to the Church and to the world of the deep, rich, feminine perspective. How unfortunate the implied collusion of the Church with the world in gender-oppressive actions that flow from such attitudes. If we are ever to effect a shift toward a more just and necessarily more inclusive reality, we must offer a systemic challenge in the arena of religious ritual, with all of the theological implications that such an approach implies. It is not enough to rewrite the rules and rearrange ritual roles. We must examine our understanding of God. With courage and with love, we must expand our religious images, open up our metaphors, and make sure that our God-language is representative of all. Because *WomanPrayer, WomanSong* prays and sings out of and into women's life experience, its ritual images, metaphors, and language are bound to challenge our biblical and theological presuppositions and our understanding of Christian tradition. Let us remember, however, that these images and metaphors are deeply rooted in that very tradition. They are brought forward here in order that our tradition might continue to have meaning for women and to ensure its transmission to future generations through our daughters as well as our sons.

In all the years that I have participated in Christian liturgy, I have never once heard the institutional Church address our God as Mother, nor have I heard preached from the pulpit a biblically based homily or sermon on the feminine dimension of the Divine. We pray to God our Father. We place our trust in "Him." In the Church, male characteristics dominate our perceptions and language of God. Indeed, God's male child, Jesus, whom we call Son of God, who calls himself Son of Man, whom we address as Lord of Lords, King of Kings, Prince of Peace, whom we worship as God incarnate, is perceived by many in the Church to be the embodiment of a masculine God. Theologians will insist, and rightly, that we cannot attribute gender to our Creator God, that "Father" describes a relationship, that finite language lacks the capacity to describe the Infinite, that any attempt to name the Unknown is conditional and relative. Yet few will expand the vocabulary to include "Mother" as a metaphor for God, or any other appellation focusing on the feminine. Consequently, popular piety has missed the fine theological point that our God is *like* a Father, that "Father" is essentially a metaphor and not a designation specifying the gender of God. Why is it so difficult to call upon God our Mother? Because most Christians have concluded long ago that the God who is "Father" is male. This orientation toward God as male does have a scriptural basis, yet the Bible also speaks of a God who feeds and clothes, who nurtures and cleanses, who is protective and compassionate, who is sometimes pregnant, sometimes a midwife, who gives birth, and who suckles a child at the breast. From this feminine force flows a creative, unconditional power to bestow and sustain life. Where are the names that address this reality? Where is the language that expresses this imagery? What is missing from traditional Christianity is the theological development of the feminine face of God based on these biblical assertions and the corresponding use of feminine God-language and images in worship. Never to name or celebrate the feminine aspect of God is to disparage everything feminine. Never to hear the Word speak specifically to women is to devalue woman's worth. Never to shape our ritual in a distinctively feminine fashion implies that it is wrong to do so. Until we are touched by the transformative power of such ritual, we will not know what we are missing, not only women, but also men.

When referring to God, Christianity uses exclusively male pronouns, thereby assuming and imaging a masculine God. If you want to test the validity of anyone's claim to inclusivity, try referring to God as She. Then only will you discover the limits accorded inclusive language. A colleague, male, unwilling to call God Mother because it would be exclusive, said, "Let's just call Him It." It is deeply painful for many people to admit to the feminine in God. Neutral nouns and pronouns offer such people an alternative to facing the issue of exclusion. By addressing God in feminine terms, we help the Church resist the temptation to recreate God in the image of man, thereby setting the stage for insisting that it is in fact man, the male, who is created in the image of God, and that fathers and sons are privileged heirs to the legacy of the Father and the Son. Men may insist we women are also "sons" of God and that all of us are "brothers," but we long to be known as the daughters of God and sisters of one another, and we are painfully aware of how quickly the generic "men" can become gender-specific.

We have lessons yet to learn from the humanity and the incarnate divinity of Jesus. Perhaps God specifically took flesh as a man in order to witness to the value of the feminine, to teach men, through Jesus, that affirming the feminine is compatible with being a man, to teach us all, women and men, that true mutuality, true equality, is the core of the gospel's good news. The fact that Jesus was male does not limit God's Word to gender-specific flesh. The Word became human in order to lift up all humanity. The Resurrection reminds us not to attribute characteristics of the historical Jesus to the eschatological Christ, who transcends all limitations of gender, all limitations of culture, all limitations of flesh itself and, in a truly inclusive Spirit, continues to come again. Let us never forget that the eternal God is neither male nor female but Mystery, a Presence, Power, Love. Underlying the rituals of *WomanPrayer, WomanSong* is the effort to overcome the limitations of language to come to this understanding of God.

It is not going to be easy to alter our perception of the Judeo-Christian God. When I shared with a colleague, a biblical scholar, my resetting of the Genesis account of creation to reflect a feminine understanding of God, he was genuinely appreciative of my efforts but thought I was referring to Tiamat, the goddess of the ancient Near East. What we know of our God has come down to us in the context of a tradition chronicled in scripture, a tradition that has insisted God is male. Only recently have we come to appreciate the human factor in the written records and their transmission, and it no longer seems unreasonable to suggest that the revealed word of God, contained in texts recorded by men, edited by men, canonized by men, translated by men, interpreted by men, and until recently preached upon exclusively by men, might have a patriarchal bias. The biblical scholar Elisabeth Schüssler Fiorenza invites us to approach the texts of the Bible with a hermeneutic of suspicion (see her book *In Memory of Her*), and most feminist theologians endorse a hermeneutic of experience as critical to understanding these texts. There is no other way that women, generally excluded from the canonical writings, will find their place within the tradition. Behind the received texts, behind the written records, is a history of women's experience preserved in an oral tradition that has been completely overshadowed. It is here that women, guided by the Holy Spirit, are seeking to find meaning and affirmation from the God of their own tradition and to give voice to what God reveals.

Behind all of my use of scripture is an effort to be faithful to the essential spirit of God's Revelation embodied in the texts, even as the texts struggle to be an authentic word of God for all human beings, women and men. This hermeneutic of fidelity is informed by the insights of biblical scholarship, some arising from historical-critical exegesis, others from liberation theology or a feminist theology. At times these discoveries have held up a new perspective for ritual reenactment, at other times they have led me to question the validity of a translation or the very nature of the original event.

For example, contemporary scholars suggest that the coming of the Magi, recorded only by Matthew, may never have actually happened but may simply represent a theological narrative constructed to make a point. If so, then what is the point? Women bring a different set of questions to bear upon such a text, resulting in different insights and very often different meanings. It may be that the central message lies not in the dramatic act of worship of the wealthy and prestigious Magi but in the silence of the mother and the vulnerability of her Child. In "Come, Spirit" I suggest we link the first two chapters of the Book of Acts, moving directly from verse fourteen of chapter one to verse one of chapter two, a logical connection. We would see immediately that women were among those who were gathered when the Spirit descended in tongues of flame to shake not only the foundations of the house but the very structure of society, for women also preached in tongues, together with the men, proclaiming the beginning of a new age in the spirit of

Jesus the Christ. Sometimes a simple editorial shift will open up for women an avenue into the heart of God's loving, liberating word.

The scripture readings in the rituals of this book reflect the conviction that God's word is essentially event, continually contemporary, open to everyone. The settings of the texts are meant to enhance the rhythmic poetry of the spoken word, so that through the sound we might feel the power of God's compelling Word. God's word is far more than words recorded in ancient books, even those that are canonical. Before there were words, the Word was God, and God spoke, and there was life. Women are searching among the words for the Word of God, a word of life. Underlying the rituals of *WomanPrayer, WomanSong* is this understanding of Revelation.

Our present experience of liturgy is very different from the liturgies of distant times. Before the scriptures were written, before the word of God became associated with a printed page, communities were actively engaged in questioning and shaping the meaning of that word in the context of their rituals. In fact the scriptures themselves record many of these encounters with God's word, chronicling centuries of human experience and energy, creativity and debate, a people's struggle to know and understand the word of God for them. Both testaments preserve songs that were written and sung, interpretations that were offered, insights that were shared. These human expressions became vehicles of grace in a celebration context, in turn impressing upon the community the importance of its beliefs. Why must only past experience be considered authoritative? We who live with the Holy Spirit as Inspiration within and among us surely have every right to add our piece to the deposit of faith. It is the function of the canon to act as curator of tradition. Liturgy's role is to add to that tradition, evoking meaning, inspiring commit-ment, encouraging all of us to carry on. Underlying the rituals of *Woman-Prayer, WomanSong* is this understanding of liturgy.

It is particularly important to women that this dimension of liturgy be recognized and understood, for it is only by an active engagement with the texts, during those rituals when we choose to use the texts, that we will uncover our connection with the past. Some are recommending we depart from the tradition as transmitted through the scriptural texts, saying there is nothing there for us. Yet these sometimes dry remnants of the past, when reconstituted by the Spirit, may prove to our surprise to be spiritually nourish-ing, revealing to us that God's Revelation always involves far more than meets the eye. What is important is that we learn once again to commune with images and metaphors and to trust our experience. Texts may be helpful starting points, but they are light years removed from originating events and our foundational myths. In authentic ritual, our understanding of God, of Revelation, and of liturgy converge on the level of intuition and are integral to each other. When God's self-disclosure is experienced, the community pro-claims and celebrates its response, witnessing to the integrity of its creedal assent by the way it orders its life.

Communities of women who meet to worship have been finding it more and more difficult to pray with integrity. We are searching for the right words to match our ritual behavior to the content of our beliefs. The recent insights of feminist theology, the power of our shared experience, and the witness of so many dedicated lives have led to a hunger for new worship language and new worship images, new songs and new celebrations that will be for us appropriate prayer and praise. *WomanPrayer, WomanSong*, a collection of ritual resources prepared from a feminine perspective, shatters the ritual silence surrounding the Divine Feminine in traditional Christian worship as it encourages women to claim their place at the heart of creation, the Church, and human society and to joyfully celebrate that claim. While these rituals have been designed primarily for women, they are open also to men, particularly those men sensitive to the suffering of women, who support their struggle for justice, and who sometimes pray with them. When men and women are present, adjust the texts to reflect inclusive language, or invite the men to experience firsthand what it is like to worship when they feel excluded. Raising awareness experientially may help prepare the way for a more inclusive religious reality for both women and men.

It is important to affirm the distinction between primary rites and supplementary rituals. What is offered here is an alternative in addition to official worship, with the hope that our celebrational lives will be enriched by our coming together more often to pray. The themes focus on integral values, seeking to reveal the rhythms of the universe that beat in the human heart.

If the world is to survive the violence and desecration of a self-centered, technological age, it must take women seriously. Through *Creation Rituals*, we awaken to the feminine in the universe as we encounter "El Shaddai" (a title for God occurring some forty times in the Hebrew scriptures and sometimes translated as "the breasted one") and learn to call God by another name. As we visit again the basic elements of life—earth, air, water, fire—we perceive a little more clearly how all creation mirrors the feminine face of God, a God who is Mystery.

Liturgical tradition has conditioned us to a prescribed way of seeing, namely, through the patriarchal eye. Focusing on the primary liturgical seasons, *Liberation Rituals* seek to free the feminine in worship by presenting the Word within the biblical word as the source of womanly wisdom in the seasons of Advent, Christmas, Lent, Easter, and Pentecost.

*Transformation Rituals* embrace feminine experience in the past and in the present by moving through death to life in every woman's here and now, affirming her strengths, calling her out of exile, marking time, as the circle of love spirals out and out like a wide open, welcoming wing, inviting all, women and men, to stand in the blessing of God.

Each of the eighteen themes is an independent ritual. Celebrate each ritual just as it is, or rearrange its component resources into patterns of your own. Incorporate a song or a prayer into a traditional worship service, or choose your own theme, using selections appropriate to the occasion, the group that is assembled, and the length of time available for prayer. Shorten the lengthy litanies prepared in praise of women, or put them all together as the core of an entire service, adding other names from history or from your own experience, thereby witnessing to our vast and precious heritage of heroines and saints. Be sensitive to the setting. Add a candle, flowers, a piece of pottery, a banner, an icon, or a symbol related to the theme. Arrange the chairs in a way that supports what you are hoping to achieve. A circle encourages sharing, leaving no one out. Most of the rituals were designed for small, interactive groups. Make adjustments for larger contexts, and use only what will work. Some rituals are environmental. Try locating the creation rituals outside—by a river, around a campfire—where the symbols of water or fire and flame come dramatically alive. Feel free to rearrange everything, particularly ritual roles. Responsive prayers that call for alternating sides of a congregation can be done effectively by two readers, or by the leader and the congregation, or by a reader and a choir.

The songs have their own stories and arise from my soul's sojourn among people around the globe. Bring to them your own heart's journey, sing into them your own spirit, so that meanings I have never imagined can be captured and brought to light. Their texts have been presented as poetry and prayer on the pages adjacent to the music, so that those of you who do not sing might enjoy their verbal rhythms or, once you have learned the melodies, sing directly from the texts. Songbooks for group singing, an accompaniment edition, and cassettes of the songs in this collection (entitled *WomanSong I* and *WomanSong II*) will be available by the fall of 1987.

Several of the songs and prayers used in these rituals have appeared in previous publications. My thanks to Simon & Schuster, Inc., for permission to cite John Lame Deer's reflection on circles in the ritual "Circle of Love" on page 191 (from *Lame Deer: Seeker of Visions*, copyright © 1972 by John Fire/Lame Deer and Richard Erdoes). I found the following resources especially helpful in preparing the litanies on women: *The Dinner Party* by Judy Chicago (1979); *Sisterhood Is Global*, edited by Robin Morgan (1984); *The International Dictionary of Women's Biography*, edited by Jennifer S. Uglow (1982); as well as the Old and New Testaments of the Bible. I am indebted to my Native American sisters and brothers for the concept of the Prayer of the Six Directions, integral to the spirituality of so many Indian traditions.

I am particularly grateful to Meinrad Craighead, whose artistic interpretation gave these rituals and songs a visual and deeper dimension, and to Carla DeSola, founder and director of the Omega Liturgical Dance Company, who danced two songs to life. Thank you to my new friends at Meyer•Stone Books: Pamela Johnson, for her sensitivity in preparing the manuscript for publication; Dikkon Eberhart, who saw the book's potential and encouraged its completion; and David Meyer, for his decision to publish. Thank you to my old friends, men and women around the world, to the members of my community of Medical Mission Sisters, especially Mary Elizabeth Johnson, a truly valiant woman. Your unconditional love and support is essential to my giving. This book is my gift to you.

# RITUALS

# CREATION RITUALS

## Awakening to the Feminine in the Universe

All creation
mirrors
the feminine face
of God.

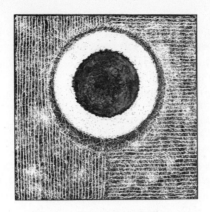

# EL SHADDAI

**ALL SING**

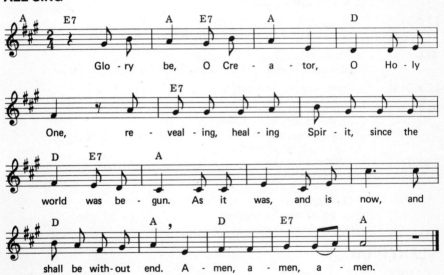

Glo - ry be, O Cre - a - tor, O Ho - ly One, re - veal - ing, heal - ing Spir - it, since the world was be - gun. As it was, and is now, and shall be with - out end. A - men, a - men, a - men.

**LEADER**     Glory to God in the highest,
and peace to all people on earth.
Mother of mercy,
we worship You,
we praise You for Your glory.

| ALL SING | Glory be, O Creator, O Holy One, revealing, healing Spirit since the world was begun. As it was, and is now, and shall be without end. Amen, amen, amen! |
|---|---|
| LEADER | Glory to God all around us, bringing good things to birth. Mother of life, we give You thanks, we praise Your steadfast love. |
| ALL SING | Glory be, O Creator, O Holy One, revealing, healing Spirit since the world was begun. As it was, and is now, and shall be without end. Amen, amen, amen! |
| LEADER | Glory to God within us, source of grace and peace. Mother of love, we look to You, we praise Your holy name. |
| ALL SING | Glory be, O Creator, O Holy One, revealing, healing Spirit, since the world was begun. As it was, and is now, and shall be without end. Amen, amen, amen! |
| LEADER | Blessed be God, our Mother. Blessed be Her name forever! |
| ALL | Blessed be God, our Mother. Blessed be Her name forever! |
| LEADER | Together let us pray: |
| ALL | Our Mother, on earth and in heaven: holy is Your name. May Your wisdom come, Your will be done, here and now, as it was in the beginning. Our Mother, on earth and in heaven: holy is Your name. |

## SILENT PRAYER

| READER | Zion said: God has forsaken me, God has forgotten me. Thus says El Shaddai: Does a woman forget the babe at her breast, or fail to nurture the child of her womb? Yet even if these do forget, I will never forget you.   *(Is 49:14-15)* |
|---|---|

| | |
|---|---|
| **LEADER** | Let us give thanks and rejoice: |
| **ALL** | We give thanks for having touched this day the feminine face of God. |

## SILENT PRAYER

**READER**    Listen, offspring of Rachel,
survivors of the House of Israel,
whom I have carried
from the day you were born.
Into old age will I be with you,
unto grey hair will I support you.
As I have done,
so will I do.
I have carried you,
and I will deliver you.   *(Is 46:3-4)*

**LEADER**    Let us give thanks and rejoice:

**ALL**    We give thanks for having touched this day the feminine face of God.

## SILENT PRAYER

**READER**    O Jerusalem, Jerusalem,
killing the prophets,
stoning those who are sent to you!
How I have longed to gather your children,
as a hen with her chicks under her wings,
and you refused.   *(Mt 23:37)*
Thus says El Shaddai:
Have I not pleaded with you
as a mother might plead with her daughters
or a father with his sons
or a nurse with her children,
that you should be my people
and that I should be your God,
that you are my daughters and sons,
and I am mother and father to you?
I have gathered you as a hen gathers
her brood under her wings.   *(2 Esdras 1:28-30)*

**LEADER**    Let us give thanks and rejoice:

**ALL**    We give thanks for having touched this day the feminine face of God.

## SILENT PRAYER

**READER**    As one whom a mother comforts,
so will I comfort you.   *(Is 66:13)*
Like newborn babies,
crave the milk
of spiritual honesty,
so that you might mature
toward your salvation,

> now that you have tasted
> the goodness of God.  *(1 Pet 2:2-3)*

**LEADER**  Let us give thanks and rejoice:

**ALL**  We give thanks for having touched this day
the feminine face of God.

## SILENT PRAYER

**LEADER**  In traditional Christian piety, in theology and liturgy, God is
depicted as male. In Christian spirituality, we address
God as our Father. But God is neither male nor female.
God transcends all categories, although both feminine
and masculine qualities shape what we know of God.
To enumerate is to fall into the trap of gender-related
stereotypes. Let it suffice to say:

The God of history,
the God of the Bible,
is One who carries us in Her arms
after carrying us in Her womb,
breastfeeds us,
nurtures us,
teaches us how to walk,
teaches us how to soar upward
just as the eagle teaches its young
to stretch their wings and fly,
makes fruitful,
brings to birth,
clothes the lilies of the field,
clothes Eve and Adam with garments newmade,
clothes you and me
with skin and flesh
and a whole new level of meaning
with the putting on of Christ.

The God of tradition,
the canonical God,
is One who cares about people,
who values personal relationships,
who walks with,
talks with,
listens to
demanding, complaining friends,
is willing to negotiate,
is patient
and merciful,
provides shelter
and a homeland,
security
and roots.

The God of scripture,
the living God,

is One who feeds the hungry,
heals the brokenhearted,
binds up all their wounds,
comforts as a mother comforts,
gathers Her brood protectively
to Her safe and sheltering wing.
God-with-us
is the Word-made-flesh,
steadfast love,
mother-love,
love incarnate,
the love one has
for a child in the womb,
on whom we depend
like a child in the womb,
in whom we live
and move
and have our being,
the Holy
and wholly Other.
So why shouldn't we
as the Spirit moves
sometimes call God
Mother?

**ALL SING**    "Mother and God" (See page 207.)

## SILENT REFLECTION

**LEADER**    And so we pray
in the Spirit of Jesus:
Mother,
that all may be one,
as You are in me
and I am in You,
that they may be one
as we are one.
With me in them
and You in me,
with me in You
and them in me,
may we be so completely one
that the world will know for certain,
Mother,
that You have sent me
and have loved them
as much as You love me.   *(Jn 17:21-23)*

**LEADER**    Blessed be God, our Mother.
Blessed be Her name forever!

**ALL**    Blessed be God, our Mother.
Blessed be Her name forever!

## REFLECTION / SHARING

*Reflect on how you feel about addressing God as Mother, and why you feel that way.*

*After reflecting quietly for a time, form small groups, and share with one another the fruit of your reflection.*

*Time permitting, share your predominant image of God and why that image is or is not meaningful for you.*

**LEADER**    Blessed be God, our Mother.
Blessed be Her name forever!

**ALL**    Blessed be God, our Mother.
Blessed be Her name forever!

**LEADER**    Together let us pray:

**ALL**    Our Mother,
on earth and in heaven:
holy is Your name.
May Your wisdom come,
Your will be done,
here and now,
as it was in the beginning,
and will be forever.
Amen.

## BENEDICTION

**LEADER**    May you walk with God
**ALL**    May you walk with God

**LEADER**    in the daily unfolding,
**ALL**    in the daily unfolding,

**LEADER**    in the sharp pain of growing,
**ALL**    in the sharp pain of growing,

**LEADER**    in the midst of confusion,
**ALL**    in the midst of confusion,

**LEADER**    in the bright light of knowing.
**ALL**    in the bright light of knowing.

**LEADER**    May you live in God,
**ALL**    May you live in God,

**LEADER**    in Her constant compassion,
**ALL**    in Her constant compassion,

**LEADER**    may yours increase,
**ALL**    may yours increase,

**LEADER**    in Her infinite wisdom,
**ALL**    in Her infinite wisdom,

| LEADER | in Her passion for peace. |
|--------|---------------------------|
| ALL | in Her passion for peace. |
| LEADER | May you walk with God |
| ALL | May you walk with God |
| LEADER | and live in God |
| ALL | and live in God |
| LEADER | and remain with God |
| ALL | and remain with God |
| LEADER | forever. Amen. |
| ALL | forever. Amen. |

**SONG**       "Mother and God" (See page 207.)

*Incorporate the dance movements that follow.*

## MOTHER AND GOD

### The Dance

*Rehearse the following dance movements before the beginning of the ritual. Dance prayers work best when the song is taught first, then the gestures, and then both are put together. Repetition is important for a feeling of ease, connection, and prayer to develop.*

OPENING POSITION All are seated, with torso rounded over, arms at sides, palms facing upward. This position is held a moment to allow prayer to well up from within. Feel it coming from a deep, curved place.

*Mother and God, to You we sing:*

The torso unfolds, arms moving inward, upward, and extending forward in a circular motion. Folding over again, the motion is completed with the torso and arms in the rounded over position. This is repeated, the second time in a slightly fuller way.

*wide is Your womb, warm is Your wing.*

Arms rise, palms facing down, with a feeling of expansion. (Connect the lifting of the arms with a lifting, pulling in and contracting engagement in the torso, so that the movement has power.) The arms are then placed gently over the shoulders of the person on either side.

*In You we live, move, and are fed,*
*sweet, flowing milk, life-giving bread.*

All rock slowly, side to side, right - left - right - left, and so forth.

*Mother and God, to You we bring*

Arms disengage by rising upward, then forward and inward, ending close to the torso, body curved over as in the first movement *(Mother and God)*. The right hand extends forward, palm facing up, followed by the left hand placed on the right, both palms facing upward. This is done with an intention of offering *(to You we bring)*.

*all broken hearts, all broken wings.*

Hands draw inward and are placed over the heart, with the torso slightly rounded, and a feeling of reverence *(all broken hearts)*. Hands stretch sideways, right hand to the left, left hand to the right, and clasp the hands of the person on either side *(all broken wings)*. Pause.

The entire pattern is repeated, standing.

*Choreography by Carla DeSola*
*Omega Liturgical Dance Company*

# MOTHER EARTH

*Gather in a circle. In the center of the circle, or in a prominent place if the assembly is too large for a circle, artfully arrange a representative sampling of the gifts of the earth, such as these:*

- *a bowl of flowers*
- *dry twigs, leafy branches*
- *leaves, according to climate and season*
  - *... dry, brittle, brightly colored, green*
- *rocks, small stones*
- *uprooted weeds with roots exposed*
- *a container of soil*
- *a container of water*
- *fruits, nuts, seeds*

## ENTERING INTO SILENCE

*Listen to "Return to Gaia" from Paul Winter's Missa Gaia/Earth Mass (available on cassette) and try to experience your own connection to the earth, our mother.*

**READER**   In the beginning,
in the very beginning,
God gave birth to,
God delivered,
God created
the heavens and the earth.
Yes, out of the womb
of fertile divinity
emerged our mother,
the earth.

**ALL SING**     *Very slowly*

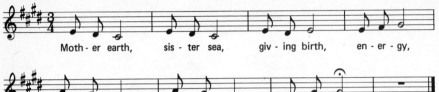

Moth - er earth,     sis - ter sea,     giv - ing birth,     en - er - gy,

reach - ing out,     touch - ing me     lov - ing - ly.

Miriam Therese Winter
Copyright © Medical Mission Sisters, 1987

**READER**     The earth was formless
and empty.
There was darkness
over the deep.
God paused,
reflected.
Her brooding spirit
hovered
restless
over the face of the waters,
savoring the stillness,
embracing the mystical moment,
contemplating the indissoluble cord
binding Her to the earth.

**ALL SING**     Mother earth, sister sea, giving birth, energy,
reaching out, touching me lovingly.

**READER**     God loved
the fruit of Her womb
with all its potential for good.
Intuitively,
She broke the silence,
singing:
Let there be light!
Her sunlight chased the shadows.
She danced with the moon and the stars.
She sang all life into being:
seeds, trees,
fruits and flowers,
birds that took to the heavens
and creatures that kept to the earth.
She taught earth all about motherhood,
about nurture,
about birth.

**ALL SING**     Mother earth, sister sea, giving birth, energy,
reaching out, touching me lovingly.

**READER**    God sang:
Let there be life
fashioned in My image.
She created humankind
in Her image,
rational beings
She created them,
female and male
She created them,
from out of the earth
She created them.
From humus of earth,
from mud, from muck,
She fashioned in Her image
woman
and man,
breathed into them
Her spirit,
the very breath of life.
From the beginning,
humankind
is the love child of our God
in the womb of mother earth.

*(Creation Accounts in Genesis)*

**ALL SING**    Mother earth, sister sea, giving birth, energy,
reaching out, touching me lovingly.

**READER**    In the very first days,
in the very first nights,
in the earliest years,
in the earliest light,
when everything needed was brought into being,
when everything was properly named and nourished,
when bread was baked in the shrines of earth,
when bread was broken in the homes of earth,
God looked upon Her handiwork
and saw that it was good.   *(Sumerian Cycle of Inanna)*

**ALL SING**    "Mother Earth" (Sing entire song, page 209.)

**LEADER**    Humus:
    the brown, black substance
    formed from decomposing matter;
    the organic portion of the soil;
    the basic stuff of life.
Humor:
    bodily fluids and secretions,
    the juices of animate life;
    a sense of the absurd;
    response to the incongruous;
    the ability to laugh.

Human:
    having the characteristics of a living person;
    capable of relationship, comprehension, motivation;
    unpredictable and fallible.
Humility:
    modest, self-effacing;
    aware that one comes from and returns to
    the humus of the earth.
We humans
share genetic qualities
with humility,
and laughter,
and life.
We have a lot in common
with compost
and with earth.
We are destined
to decompose
like autumn leaves,
like rotting fruit,
we who are children of God
and siblings of the stars.
Reason enough to be humble
when confronted by our own creativity,
or when tempted to pretentious arrogance,
reason enough to laugh.

## SILENT REFLECTION

*Spend a few minutes reflecting quietly on who you are and how you feel*
> • *as a woman*
> • *at this time in your life.*
*Why do you feel as you do?*

*When you are able to identify your feelings, get up and select from the centerpiece arrangement something that symbolizes your feelings: a dry twig, a flower, an uprooted plant, a stone.*

*Return to your seat and contemplate the symbol, relating its characteristics to your own sense of yourself. As you hold this earth gift in your hand, try to draw energy from its essential dynamism and strength from its inner truth.*

## SHARED REFLECTION

*If you wish, share briefly with the group how you feel as a woman, why you chose your particular symbol, how it seems to mirror who you are.*

## SHARED PRAYER

*When the personal reflections have ended, move immediately into informal, shared prayer. Pray aloud spontaneously for that special grace to meet your present need. Use images evoked by your symbol. Pray for yourself or for someone else in the group who may be especially in need of prayer.*

**LEADER**    Let us pray:
Blessed be God
for the many gifts
of divine maternity,
for the newness of life
and the nurture
we experience day after day.
Blessed be the full
and faithful breasts
of our birth mother earth.
May we cherish her
and the fruits of her womb
as our God cherishes us.
Blessed be the human spirit,
an innately holy spirit,
that enables earth's capacities
to claim beatitude.
Blessed be God,
Sustainer of life,
now and forever. Amen.

**SONG**    "Mother Earth" (Refrain; last verse; refrain; page 209)

# BREATH OF GOD

*Sit in a circle. When all are settled and quiet, the Leader begins by tapping a slow, steady beat on a small, percussion woodblock. When the Leader gives a starting signal, the group begins to synchronize its breathing. Inhale for four beats, exhale for four. When all are inhaling/exhaling rhythmically together, one person in the group strikes a triangle on the first of every four beats, at the start of the intake of breath and at the beginning of its release.*

*Eventually the Leader begins to "chant" softly as she exhales, "Breath of God..." one word per beat, holding God for the count of three and four. Spontaneously, others join in, until all are participating. There is no melody. The chant is more like a murmur, a hum, a breath of sound. It begins softly and may grow in volume as the group begins to identify with the sound and with each other. A melody, even harmony, may or may not emerge. Simply enter into the sound, the word, the breathing, until the word and the breath and you are one, and all are bound in a collective experience of being formed by the Breath of God.*

*When the experience has peaked, stop the triangle, let the chanting taper off, stop the woodblock beat. The Leader invites the group to remain centered as each returns to her normal breathing pattern. Then a Reader proclaims a Word of Good News into the centered silence.*

**READER**     When the day of Pentecost came around,
they were all together in one room.
Suddenly the sound of a rushing wind
shook the house where they were sitting,
and all were filled with the Holy Spirit.   *(Ac 2:1-2,4)*

| LEADER | Jesus breathed on them and said: |
|---|---|
| ALL | "Receive the Holy Spirit!"  *(Jn 20:22)* |
| LEADER | Jesus breathed on them and said: |
| ALL | "Receive the Holy Spirit!" |
| LEADER | Jesus breathed on them and said: |
| ALL | "Receive the Holy Spirit!" |
| ALL SING | "Breath of God" |

*Begin with a flute or another woodwind instrument. Play the melody through once. If no instrument is available, have a group member sing the melody without words, on the syllable "oo." After hearing the melody once, all join in. Repeat the piece three times.*

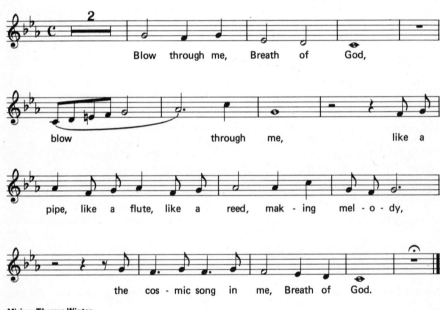

Blow through me, Breath of God, blow through me, like a pipe, like a flute, like a reed, mak - ing mel - o - dy, the cos - mic song in me, Breath of God.

Miriam Therese Winter
Copyright © Medical Mission Sisters, 1987

| READER | The hand of God was upon me, |
|---|---|
| | and She transported me |
| | by the Spirit |
| | and set me in the middle of a valley, |
| | a valley full of bones. |
| | She made me walk among them, |
| | a whole valley full of bones, |
| | and they were very dry. |
| | "Daughter, can these bones live?" |
| | She asked. |
| | "You should know, Shaddai," |
| | I answered. |

Then She said to me:
"Prophesy over these bones;
say to them,
O dry bones,
hear the word of God!
Thus says El Shaddai to these bones:
I shall fill you with breath,
and you will live.
I will put sinews and flesh upon you,
and cover you with skin,
and put breath in you,
and you shall live,
and you shall know that I am God."
So I prophesied as I was commanded;
and as I prophesied,
there was a loud noise,
a clattering sound,
and the bones came together,
bone to bone.
I looked and saw
that they were covered with sinews,
they were covered with flesh,
they were covered with skin,
but there was no breath in them.
"Prophesy to the breath, daughter,
prophesy and say to the breath,
Thus says El Shaddai:
Come from the four winds,
Come, O breath,
and breathe upon these dead,
that they may live again!"
So I prophesied as God had commanded,
and the breath entered into them,
an immense number of them,
and they all came to life again.   *(Ez 37:1-10)*

**ALL SING**    Blow through me, Breath of God,
blow through me,
like a pipe, like a flute, like a reed,
making melody,
the cosmic song in me,
Breath of God.   *(Repeat.)*

## SILENT REFLECTION

**LEADER**    Air: fresh, clean, pervasive,
one of the four basic elements of our universe.
Breath: filling our lungs, filling our senses,
fundamental to human life.
Wind: whistling through the leaves of trees,
setting everything into motion,
a synonym for the Holy Spirit.

Reflect on Air, Breath, Wind,
on what they mean to all of life,
on what they mean to you, to me.
Air, Breath, Wind:
each is another name for God.

**ALL SING**  Blow through me, Breath of God,
blow through me,
like a pipe, like a flute, like a reed,
making melody,
the cosmic song in me,
Breath of God.

## SILENT REFLECTION

**LEADER**  Air, Breath, Wind: dynamic metaphors
that help us express
symbolically
the workings of God in us.
How is it with your heart?
  *(Pause)*

A hollow reed is a channel
for the whispering of God.
  *(Pause)*

A silent flute makes music
when blown by the breath of God.
  *(Pause)*

A breath-filled balloon
lifts, soars,
is borne aloft on currents of air
and dances in the wind.
  *(Pause)*

A kite is just a frame and string,
until the wind embraces it
and frees it to be itself.
  *(Pause)*

Trees bow before,
are buffeted by,
gales of hurricane force,
or blossom in April breezes,
or celebrate the windsong
rustling their reality.
  *(Pause)*

How is it with your heart?
What is the image that captures for you,
at this point in time,
the dynamic of God-in-you?
Are you a flute, a hollow reed?
Are you a tree in a violent storm,
or a tree in a creative season?

Are you a kite, a balloon, a bubble, a bird?
How is it with your heart?

**ALL SING**    Blow through me, Breath of God,
blow through me,
like a pipe, like a flute, like a reed,
making melody,
the cosmic song in me,
Breath of God.

## SILENT REFLECTION

## SHARED REFLECTION

*Share aloud a particular image that best symbolizes your present relationship to God, and tell why that image is appropriate for you.*

*After the sharing, sit silently until the Leader invites the community to respond with the following:*

**LEADER**    The breath of Shaddai has formed me;
**ALL**          the breath of God gives me life.   *(Job 33:4)*

**LEADER**    The breath of Shaddai has formed me;
**ALL**          the breath of God gives me life.

**LEADER**    The breath of Shaddai has formed me;
**ALL**          the breath of God gives me life.

**ALL SING**    Blow through me, Breath of God,
blow through me,
like a pipe, like a flute, like a reed,
making melody,
the cosmic song in me,
Breath of God.

**LEADER**    Let everything that breathes praise Shaddai!   *(Ps 150:6)*
**ALL**          Let everything that breathes praise Shaddai!

**READER**    God fashioned our ancestors
from the dust of the earth,
breathed into their nostrils the breath of life,
and they became living beings.   *(Gen 2:7)*

**LEADER**    Let everything that breathes praise Shaddai!
**ALL**          Let everything that breathes praise Shaddai!

**READER**    By the word of God were the heavens made,
their vast expanse by the breath of Her mouth.   *(Ps 33:6)*

**LEADER**    Let everything that breathes praise Shaddai!
**ALL**          Let everything that breathes praise Shaddai!

**READER**    In Her hand is the life of every living thing
and the breath of all humankind.   *(Job 12:10)*

**LEADER**    Let everything that breathes praise Shaddai!
**ALL**          Let everything that breathes praise Shaddai!

## BENEDICTION

**LEADER**     May God our Creator breathe into you (us)
       new life
       and a whole new meaning.
     May the Spirit of God breathe into you (us)
       a new spirit
       and a new understanding.
     May the Wisdom of God breathe into you (us)
       new hope
       and a new awareness.
     And may all who hear the Word of God
       be blessed forever.

**ALL**     Amen.

**SONG**     "Breath of God"   *(Sing twice.)*
or "Spirit of God" (From the collection, *Joy Is Like The Rain*; edited for inclusive language in *An Anthology of Scripture Songs* by Miriam Therese Winter; published by Medical Mission Sisters, Philadelphia, PA 19111.)

# LIVING WATER

Before the prayer begins, set a large glass (or pottery) bowl in a central place. Beside it set a large glass (or pottery) pitcher filled with water; a much smaller bowl; a branch of evergreen suitable for sprinkling, and several small towels.

Dim the room lights, except for a light focused on the pitcher and the empty bowl. After the assembly has settled into silence and has had time to center itself in quiet prayer, the Minister of Symbols enters, appropriately robed.

## MINISTER OF SYMBOLS

Standing directly behind the pitcher and bowl, facing the community, palms joined in a gesture of prayer, she makes a profound bow (bend forward from the waist until the upper body is parallel to the floor), then lifts the pitcher high above her head, circling slowly, clockwise, until she returns to her starting position. Then lowering the pitcher a little, she slowly pours the water into the bowl from a great height, allowing the water to fall noisily into the bowl and to splash onto the surrounding surfaces. When most of the water has been poured, she sets the pitcher down and stands with palms joined in an attitude of prayer as the community sings.

## SONG LEADER OR CHOIR

Sing "Living Water" once to establish the melody, then invite everyone to sing.

**ALL SING**

Part One

Liv - ing Wa - ter, like a riv - er, like a foun - tain, like the sea. Liv - ing Wa - ter, like a riv - er, ev - er ris - ing, rise in me.

## MINISTER OF SYMBOLS

*The Minister of Symbols is joined by an Assistant, who comes forward from the midst of the assembly. The Minister extends her hands, palms up, over the bowl, as the Assistant pours water slowly over her extended hands. The Minister rubs her hands together in a gesture of cleansing, then cups her hands, takes a sip of the water, and lets the remainder fall into the bowl. The Assistant puts down the pitcher, takes one of the towels, dries the hands of the Minister, and returns to her place. The Minister stands as before, while the community sings.*

**ALL SING**     Living Water, like a river, like a fountain, like the sea.
Living Water, like a river, ever rising, rise in me.

## MINISTER OF SYMBOLS

*The Minister dips the small bowl into the larger bowl to fill it with water, takes the tree branch, and blesses the Four Directions of the Universe (East, South, West, North) with the water, beginning with a quarter turn to her right, and concluding with a return to her original position and a sprinkling in the direction of the community. She puts the bowl and branch down and stands as before, while the community sings.*

**ALL SING**     Living Water, like a river, like a fountain, like the sea.
Living Water, like a river, ever rising, rise in me.

## MINISTER OF SYMBOLS

*Palms joined, the Minister makes a profound bow over the water, in the direction of the community, then leaves to take her place in the assembly.*

### LIVING WATER / SOURCE OF LIFE

**LEADER**     God our Mother,
Source of Life:

**ALL**        In You we live
and move
and have our being.
Glory and praise to You!

**READER**    A reading from the Book of Ezekiel, the prophet:

Then God brought me back to the entrance
of the Temple, where a stream flowed
from under its threshold,
out toward the east.
The water flowed from under the south end
of the Temple, south of the altar.
I was led out by way of the north gate,
as far as the outer east gate,
where the water was flowing south.
She moved to the east with a measuring line
and marked off a thousand cubits.
She then made me wade across the stream;
the water was ankle deep.
She measured off another thousand,
and led me through the stream again,
and the water was up to my knees.
She measured off another thousand,
led me through the stream again,
and the water was up to my waist.
She measured off another thousand,
and the stream was now a river,
which I simply could not cross.
The stream had swollen,
the water was deep,
deep enough to swim in,
a river impossible to cross.
She then said:
Daughter of woman,
do you see?
She led me back along the bank of the river,
where there were many trees on either side.
Then She said to me:
This water flows east,
down into the sea,
where it makes the stagnant sea water
fresh and wholesome again.
Wherever the river flows,
the waters will teem with life.
Fish will be plentiful,
and everything will live,
wherever the river goes.
People will fish along its banks.
In every town along its route,
they will spread out their nets.
The fish will be varied and plentiful,
like the fish of the Great Sea.
Marshes and swamps will be brackish,

but along the river, on either bank,
there will grow all kinds of trees for food.
Their leaves will never wither,
and their fruit will never fail.
Every month, they will bear fresh fruit,
because the stream that waters them
flows from the sanctuary.
Their fruit will be for food,
and their leaves will be for healing.   *(Ez 47:1-12)*

**LEADER**      God our Mother,
Source of Life:

**ALL**      In You we live
and move
and have our being.
Glory and praise to You!

**ALL SING**      Living Water, like a river, like a fountain, like the sea.
Living Water, like a river, ever rising, rise in me.

**LEADER**      Reflect quietly on how God, like a river of living water,
has been source of life for you and for the universe.

## SILENT REFLECTION

## SHARED THANKSGIVING

*If you wish, give thanks aloud for some dimension of God's life-giving presence which you have experienced, or of which you are aware. At the conclusion of the sharing, sing the following refrain.*

### SONG LEADER OR CHOIR

*Sing the refrain once to establish the melody, then invite everyone to sing.*

### ALL SING

Part Two

Miriam Therese Winter
Copyright © Medical Mission Sisters, 1976, 1987

### I WILL POUR CLEAN WATER UPON YOU

**LEADER**      God our Mother,
You wash us

and cleanse us
and come among us
as One who serves:

**ALL**    In You we live
and move
and have our being.
Glory and praise to You!

**READER**    A reading from the Gospel according to John:

Now they were at supper,
and the devil had already persuaded
Judas Iscariot to betray him.
Jesus, knowing that God
had put everything into his hands,
that he had come from God
and was returning to God,
rose from the table,
removed his outer garment,
and wrapped a towel around him.
Then he poured water into a basin
and began to wash his disciples' feet
and to wipe them with the towel.
He came to Simon Peter, who said:
"Lord, are you going to wash my feet?"
Jesus answered:
"You do not know what I am doing now,
but later you will understand."
But Peter said,
"You shall never wash my feet."
Jesus replied,
"If I do not wash you,
you have no part in me."
Simon Peter answered,
"Not only my feet,
but my hands and my head as well!"
Jesus said to him,
"Whoever has bathed does not need to wash,
except for the feet;
that person is clean all over.
You are clean,
but not all of you,"
he said,
for he knew who was to betray him.
When he had washed their feet
and put on his clothes,
he went back to his place at table
and said:
"Do you understand what I have done to you?
You call me Leader and Teacher,
and rightly,
for so I am.

If I then, your Leader and Teacher,
have washed your feet,
you also should wash each other's feet.
I have given you an example,
that you might do to one another
as I have done to you.
Truly I say to you,
no servant is greater than her mistress,
nor is she who is sent
greater than she who sent her.
Now that you know these things,
blessed are you if you do them." *(Jn 13:2-17)*

**LEADER**  God our Mother,
You wash us
and cleanse us
and come among us
as One who serves:

**ALL**  In You we live
and move
and have our being.
Glory and praise to You!

**ALL SING**  Living Water, full and free.
Living Water, live in me.

**LEADER**  I will pour clean water upon you,
says God,
and you shall be clean
from all your uncleanness;
from all your idols I will cleanse you.  *(Ez 36:25)*

**ALL**  Wash away my guilt, O God,
and cleanse me from my sin.  *(Ps 51:2)*

**LEADER**  Let us call to mind a particular failing
which we would like to have washed away.

## RITUAL CLEANSING

*The Minister of Symbols takes a large, empty bowl from a side table and is joined by her Assistant, carrying a pitcher full of water and a towel. Together they move around the circle, from person to person, washing and drying each one's hands. As the water is poured over the hands, each one says aloud:*

Wash away my guilt, O God,
and cleanse me from my sin.

*If the group is large and time is a factor, have two teams with pitchers and bowls moving in opposite directions around the circle. When the ritual is completed, place the bowl/s of tainted water near the bowl of living water, either down on the floor or off to the side.*

**ALL SING**  "Living Water" (Parts one and two together in harmony.)

Liv - ing Wa - ter, like a riv - er,

Liv - ing Wa - ter,

like a foun - tain, like the sea. Liv - ing Wa - ter,

full and free. Liv - ing

like a riv - er, ev - er ris - ing, rise in me.

Wa - ter, live in me.

Miriam Therese Winter
Copyright © Medical Mission Sisters, 1976, 1987

## WHOEVER IS THIRSTY, COME TO ME

**LEADER**    God our Mother,
Living Water
to all who thirst:

**ALL**    In You we live
and move
and have our being.
Glory and praise to You!

**READER**    A reading from the prophet Isaiah:

When the poor and the needy search for water,
and none is to be found,
and their tongues are parched with thirst,
then I, their God, will answer them;
I will not abandon them.
I will make rivers run on barren heights
and fountains in the valleys;

I will turn the wilderness into a lake
and dry land into springs of water.  *(Is 41:17-18)*

**LEADER**     Whoever is thirsty, come to Me.
Who believes in Me, come and drink.
From My breasts flow fountains of living water.  *(Jn 7:37-38)*

**ALL**     Whoever is thirsty, come to Me.
Who believes in Me, come and drink.
From My breasts flow fountains of living water.

## SILENT PRAYER

**READER**     A reading from the Gospel according to John:

On his way through Samaria,
Jesus came to the town of Sychar,
near the field that Jacob gave to Joseph, his son.
Jacob's well is there,
and Jesus, tired from his journey,
sat down beside the well.
A Samaritan woman came to draw water.
Jesus said to her,
"Give me a drink."
His disciples had gone into town
to buy food.
The woman replied,
"You, a Jew, are asking me, a Samaritan,
for a drink?"
Jews do not associate with Samaritans.
Jesus replied,
"If you only knew what God has to give,
and who it is that asks for a drink,
you would have asked of him instead,
and he would have given you living water."
The woman answered,
"You have no bucket, and the well is deep.
How can you get this living water?
Are you greater than Jacob,
who gave us this well,
and drank from it,
with his sons and his cattle?"
Jesus said to her,
"Whoever drinks this water
will thirst again;
but whoever drinks the water
that I shall give
will never thirst again;
for the water I give
becomes a spring within,
welling up to eternal life."  *(Jn 4:5-14)*

**LEADER**     Whoever is thirsty, come to Me.
Who believes in Me, come and drink.
From My breasts flow fountains of living water.

**ALL**       Whoever is thirsty, come to Me.
Who believes in Me, come and drink.
From My breasts flow fountains of living water.

## SILENT PRAYER

**LEADER**     God our Mother,
Living Water
to all who thirst:

**ALL**       In You we live
and move
and have our being.
Glory and praise to You!

## SONG LEADER OR CHOIR

*Sing the refrain once to establish the melody, then invite everyone to sing.*

**ALL SING**
           Part Three

Miriam Therese Winter
Copyright © Medical Mission Sisters, 1976, 1987

**LEADER**     In the early Church,
on occasion,
the Eucharist was celebrated
with bread and water.
As we share a cup of water
with one another,
let it be for us
a symbol of eucharist
and a sign of our solidarity
with one another in Christ.
Let us call to mind these words of Jesus:
"Whoever gives you a cup of water to drink
because you belong to Christ,
will surely receive a reward." *(Mk 9:41)*

## SHARING OF THE CUP

*The Minister of Symbols takes a large glass or cup, one that is or resembles a chalice, fills it with water from the pitcher of living water, and offers it to a member of the community, along with these words:*

> This is the cup of Living Water.
> Take and drink.

*A small towel accompanies the cup.*

*As each member takes the cup, she says "amen" to the spoken words, drinks, wipes the lip of the cup, and passes it on to another, with the words:*

> This is the cup of Living Water.
> Take and drink.

*During the passing of the cup, the community may want to sing part three of "Living Water," then repeat part one and part two, separately at first, then both parts together.*

*When the cup has been passed to everyone and returned to its place beside the bowl of living water, the community sings its three-part song.*

**ALL SING**  "Living Water" (All three parts together, page 212)

**LEADER**  Let us pray:

## SILENT PRAYER

**LEADER**  God our Mother,
Living Water,
River of Mercy,
Source of Life,
in whom we live
and move
and have our being,
who quenches our thirst,
refreshes our weariness,
bathes
and washes
and cleanses
our wounds,
be for us always
a fountain of life,
and for all the world
a river of hope
springing up in the midst
of the deserts of despair.
Honor and blessing,
glory and praise
to You forever.

**ALL**  Amen.

## BENEDICTION

**LEADER**      May the blessing of God,
Fountain of Living Water,
flow within you (us) as a river of life.
May you (we) drink deep of Her wisdom.
May you (we) never thirst again.
May you (we) go through life refreshing many,
as a sign of healing for all,
through the One who is Life eternal.

**ALL**      Amen.

**MINISTER OF SYMBOLS**

*During the Benediction, the Minister of Symbols takes the tree branch and the small bowl of water and moves through the assembly, sprinkling all, as a sign and symbol of blessing.*

**SONG**      "Living Water" (Three-part arrangement)

*Sing the entire song (sections A and B, page 212) if possible, or only section A, with which everyone is now familiar.*

# FIRE AND FLAME

*Secure a large, thick candle in a broad, deep bowl of sand. Light the candle and place the bowl on a small table or on the floor. Place a box of small, unlit candles beside the bowl. There should be one small candle for each member of the group. Gather in a circle around the large candle's light. Auxiliary room lighting should be subdued.*

**CANTOR SINGS**

Burn-ing Force, Fire and Flame: ho-ly, ho-ly is Your name.

Miriam Therese Winter
Copyright © Medical Mission Sisters, 1987

**ALL SING**     *Repeat the above refrain three times.*

**READER**     In the beginning was Fire,
and the Fire was one with Creativity:
the Fire was Creator;
and the Fire was one with Divinity:
the Fire was Divine;
and the Fire was one with the Holy One:
the Fire was God.

**ALL SING**     Burning Force, Fire and Flame:
holy, holy is Your name.

**READER**     Fire was the Source of Life.
Through Fire
all things were made:

all things are one with
the burning, searing
power and energy
of that originating Fire.
The Fire was the Source of Life,
the Fire is Life,
and that Life is the Light of all life,
a Light shining in the darkness,
never to be extinguished,
never to be overcome.

**ALL SING**      Burning Force, Fire and Flame:
holy, holy is Your name.

**READER**      The Fire became Flame
and lived among us,
accessible, visible,
filling the earth that Fire had formed,
fulfilling prophecies,
fulfilling promises,
a pervading,
protecting
Pillar of Security,
Dawn of a New Day,
Rising Sun of Justice,
Lamp of Enlightenment,
Ray of Hope
dwelling among us,
Shekinah,
the Presence,
the Passion,
Shaddai.

**ALL SING**      Burning Force, Fire and Flame:
holy, holy is Your name.

**LEADER**

*Begin the following vocal, rhythmic chant, spoken, not sung, to a four-beat
meter, in the manner of modern "rapping."*

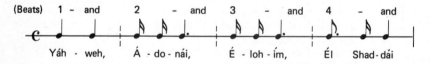

**ALL**

*Pick up the chanting, softly but intensely. Clap on downbeats (on 1, 2, 3, 4).*

*Continue chanting to provide a rhythmic, reflective base in the form of a
mantra throughout the following segment.*

*When the chanting is established, a Voice calls out loudly, over the chant-
ing, the following names or attributes of God, one name per chant phrase, or*

*each time the group chants "Yahweh." The Voice should extend as an echo over the chanting. After proclaiming a set of four names, the Voice allows the group chant to continue by itself, twice, before beginning again.*

**VOICE**      Om...

Ruach...

Allah...

Shekinah...

**ALL**      Yahweh, Adonai, Elohim, El Shaddai,
Yahweh, Adonai, Elohim, El Shaddai.

**VOICE**      Kyrie...
Pater...
Deus...
Dominus...

**ALL**      Yahweh, Adonai, Elohim, El Shaddai,
Yahweh, Adonai, Elohim, El Shaddai.

**VOICE**      Mater...
Dea...
Domina...
Sancta...

**ALL**      Yahweh, Adonai, Elohim, El Shaddai,
Yahweh, Adonai, Elohim, El Shaddai.

**VOICE**      Christus...
Christa...
Paraclitus...
Paraclita...

**ALL**      Yahweh, Adonai, Elohim, El Shaddai,
Yahweh, Adonai, Elohim, El Shaddai.

**CANTOR SINGS**   *(Sing over the chanting.)*
Burning Force, Fire and Flame:
holy, holy is Your name.

*When the moment seems right, through a gesture of invitation, encourage others to join the singing.*

**ALL SING**   *(Sing in unison until chanting ceases.)*
Burning Force, Fire and Flame:
holy, holy is Your name.

*When all have joined the singing, cease clapping, and all extend their right hand, palms down, toward the burning candle. Repeat the refrain several times, adding harmony spontaneously, as the Spirit moves.*

**LEADER**      God-with-us, a Pillar of Fire:
Blessed be God forever!

**ALL**      God-with-us, a Pillar of Fire:
Blessed be God forever!

# SILENT REFLECTION

*Lower your hands, and in the silence reflect on your experience of God as Fire.*

**READER**    Now Moses was watching over the flocks
in the wilderness
near Mount Horeb,
when a messenger of God
appeared to him
as a flame of fire
in a burning bush.
"How strange,"
said Moses,
"the bush is burning
and yet it is not consumed."
He came forward
for a closer look,
and God called to him
from the midst of the bush,
"Moses! Moses!"
"Here I am!"
said Moses;
and God replied,
"Stay where you are
and remove your shoes;
you are standing on holy ground.
I am the God of your mother,
the God of Sarah,
and Rebecca,
and Rachel;
and I am the God of your father,
the God of Abraham,
and Isaac,
and Jacob."
And Moses covered his face,
because he was afraid to look at God.   *(Ex 3:1-6)*

**LEADER**    You make fire and flame Your ministers.   *(Ps 104:4)*
Glory to You, O God!

**ALL**    You make fire and flame Your ministers.
Glory to You, O God!

**LEADER**    In a pillar of cloud,
God led the way,
in a pillar of fire,
God gave them light:
a pillar of cloud by day,
a pillar of fire by night.   *(Ex 13:21-22)*

**ALL**    You make fire and flame Your ministers.
Glory to You, O God!

**LEADER**   Who goes before You,
a devouring fire,
is Adonai, Elohim, Shaddai.   *(Dt 9:3)*

**ALL**   You make fire and flame Your ministers.
Glory to You, O God!

**LEADER**   There are three insatiable things,
four that never say, "Enough!":
Sheol, the barren womb,
the thirsting earth,
and the fire,
which never says, "Enough."   *(Prov 30:15-16)*

**ALL**   You make fire and flame Your ministers.
Glory to You, O God!

**CANTOR SINGS**

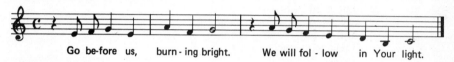

Go be-fore us,   burn - ing bright.   We will fol - low   in Your light.

Miriam Therese Winter
Copyright © Medical Mission Sisters, 1987

**ALL SING**

*Repeat the above refrain three times.*

## SILENT PRAYER

**READER**   At daybreak on the third day
a thick cloud covered the mountain;
there was thunder
and lightening
and a loud trumpet blast,
and inside the camp
the people trembled.
Moses led the people out of the camp
to the foot of the mountain
to meet God.
The mountain of Sinai was hidden in smoke,
because God had descended upon it
in fire.
The smoke rose up like the smoke of a kiln,
and the whole mountain quaked.
The sound of the trumpet
grew louder and louder.
God had come down upon Mount Sinai,
and God called Moses
to the top of the mountain,
and Moses went up to the top of the mountain,
and a cloud covered
the glory of God.

Now the glory of God
was like a devouring fire
on the top of the mountain
in the sight of all.
Moses entered the cloud
and went up the mountain
and remained on the mountain
forty days and forty nights.   *(Ex 19:16-20; 24:15-18)*

**LEADER**     The voice of God flings flames of fire,
and everything cries: Glory!   *(Ps 29:7,9)*

**ALL**     The voice of God flings flames of fire,
and everything cries: Glory!

**LEADER**     Under God's glory
a burning will be kindled,
like a consuming fire.
The light of Israel
will become a fire,
and its Holy One a flame;
it will burn and devour
thorns and briars,
all in a single day.   *(Is 10:16-17)*

**ALL**     The voice of God flings flames of fire,
and everything cries: Glory!

**LEADER**     Suddenly, without warning,
God will visit you
with thunder
and whirlwind
and earthquake
and storm
and the flame of a devouring fire.   *(Is 29:5-6)*

**ALL**     The voice of God flings flames of fire,
and everything cries: Glory!

**CANTOR SINGS**
Go before us, burning bright.
We will follow in Your light.

**ALL SING**     Go before us, burning bright.
We will follow in Your light.

## SILENT PRAYER

**READER**     Thus says Shaddai,
who created you
and formed you:
"Do not be afraid,
I have redeemed you.
I have called you by your name,
you are Mine.
Should you walk through the water,
I am with you;

rivers will not overwhelm you.
Should you walk through the fire,
you will not be burned,
and the flames will not consume you.
For I am Shaddai, the Holy One,
your Protector, and your God." *(Is 43:1-3)*

**LEADER**  I have come to cast fire upon the earth;
how I wish it were already kindled! *(Lk 12:49)*

**ALL**  I have come to cast fire upon the earth;
how I wish it were already kindled!

**LEADER**  "I baptize you with water,"
said John,
"but the One who comes
will baptize you
with the Holy Spirit
and with fire." *(Lk 3:16)*

**ALL**  I have come to cast fire upon the earth;
how I wish it were already kindled!

**LEADER**  They were all together
in one place,
when suddenly
what seemed like
tongues of fire
hovered above
each one of them,
and they were filled
with the Holy Spirit. *(Acts 2:1,3)*

**ALL**  I have come to cast fire upon the earth;
how I wish it were already kindled!

**LEADER**  Let us cherish the grace
we have been given,
let us worship God
in acceptable ways:
for our God is a consuming fire. *(Heb 12:28-29)*

**ALL**  I have come to cast fire upon the earth;
how I wish it were already kindled!

**ALL SING**  Burning Force, Fire and Flame:
holy, holy is Your name.
Go before us, burning bright.
We will follow in Your light.

*Both refrains form a single unit. Sing them together, in succession, two times.*

**LEADER**  The prophets
and all the saints of God
were on fire
with the love of God,

burned with concern
for the things
of God,
for the words
and the ways
and the will of God.
You and I,
are we on fire?
Do we burn with zeal
for compassion,
for justice?
Perhaps we burn
with anger,
with rage,
because life
is unfair.
Perhaps we harbor
a burning resentment
or disappointment
or sorrow.
Reach deep within your silent source
to touch that part of you that burns,
and call it by its name.

## REFLECTION / ACTION

*Sit silently, reflecting on whatever it is that burns within you. It may be a passion already kindled, or one you would like to fan into flame. When you have identified the burning, get up from your seat and move to the center of the circle. Take an unlit candle from the supply that is there, light it from the central flame, and return with it to your seat.*

*When everyone is settled with a lighted candle, go clockwise around the circle, beginning with the Leader, and name aloud that for or with which you burn. After each person's statement, all respond:*

**ALL**          Glory to You, O God!

*When the sharing is completed, all stand with their candles, and sing.*

**ALL SING**     Burning Force, Fire and Flame:
holy, holy is Your name.
Go before us, burning bright.
We will follow in Your light.

*As the singing continues, move forward to the center and place your candle in the sand surrounding the main candle to create a tableau of fire and flame.*

**LEADER**       Let us pray:

## SILENT PRAYER

**LEADER**       God of glory,
Your word is like a fire,
like a hammer splitting rock.   *(Jer 23:29)*

Your word in me
is a burning fire,
burning in my heart,
imprisoned in my bones,
and I am weary
with holding it in.   *(Jer 20:8-9)*
Let it burst from me
like fire and flame
to transform the earth
and all its people
to the glory of Your name.
To You Shaddai,
to You Adonai,
be glory and praise,
celebration and song,
forever and ever.

**ALL**      Amen.

**SONG**     "You, God, Are My Firmament" (See page 215.)

# MYSTERY

## ENTERING INTO SILENCE

**LEADER**    As we come together now, let us settle into stillness.
*(Pause)*

Slowly, ever so slowly, we center our minds and our hearts.
*(Pause)*

Let your cares and your weariness fall away.
*(Pause)*

Enter deeply into silence.
*(Pause)*

We are one with the universe.
*(Pause)*

We are one with the sun and the stars.
*(Pause)*

We are one with the One who is Mystery,
who created the heavens and the earth.
*(Pause)*

We are one with the One who is Mystery,
who created you and me.
*(Pause)*

O marvelous mystery!
I am one with the One who is Mystery,
the One who created me,
and loves me,
and whose Spirit lives in me.
*(Pause)*

Listen now to a song about the One who is **Mystery**,
and let its music sing in your heart.

**SONG**          "Mystery" (See page 216.)

*Listen to the song from* WomanSong *(available on cassette), or have a
soloist or the choir sing it.*

## SILENT REFLECTION

**LEADER**     O the depth
               of the riches
               and the wisdom
               and the knowledge of God!
               How incomprehensible Her judgements!
               How mysterious Her ways!

**ALL**        Who can know the mind of God?
               Who could ever be Her counselor?   *(Rm 11:33-34)*

## SILENT PRAYER

**LEADER**     From the heart of the whirlwind,
               God speaks:

**READER**     "Where were you when I laid
               the foundations
               of the earth?
               Tell me, where were you?
                 *(Pause)*

               Who decided its dimensions?
               Who laid its cornerstone,
               when all the morning stars sang,
               and all God's children
               shouted for joy?
                 *(Pause)*

               Who set the sea
               behind closed doors,
               when its waters poured forth
               from the womb?
               Who clothed it
               in a cloud of mist
               and swaddled it in darkness?
               Who set the bounds
               it could not cross,
               restraining it behind a wall?"   *(Job 38:1-11)*
                 *(Pause)*

**LEADER**     O the depth
               of the riches
               and the wisdom
               and the knowledge of God!
               How incomprehensible Her judgements!
               How mysterious Her ways!

| ALL | Who can know the mind of God?<br>Who could ever be Her counselor? |
|-----|--------|

## SILENT PRAYER

| READER | "Have you ever been in charge<br>of morning?<br>Have you ever had to summon<br>the dawn,<br>command it to cling<br>to the edges of earth<br>and shake the wicked<br>from its fold?<br>*(Pause)*<br><br>Have you ever been to the source<br>of the sea,<br>or walked in the silence<br>of the deep?<br>*(Pause)*<br><br>Have you ever seen<br>the deep, deep dark?<br>Have the gates of death<br>been shown to you?<br>Can you find your way<br>to the dwelling of light,<br>trace the pathway<br>to its home?"   *(Job 38:12-21)*<br>*(Pause)* |
|--------|--------|
| LEADER | O the depth<br>of the riches<br>and the wisdom<br>and the knowledge of God!<br>How incomprehensible Her judgements!<br>How mysterious Her ways! |
| ALL | Who can know the mind of God?<br>Who could ever be Her counselor? |

## SILENT PRAYER

| READER | "Have you any idea<br>of earth's expanse?<br>Have you been to the storehouse<br>of hail and snow?<br>*(Pause)*<br><br>Who unleashes thunder?<br>Who tells lightning<br>when to flash<br>and fling its sparks<br>upon the land?<br>Who carves a channel |
|--------|--------|

for the rain
to drench the desert's
barren wastes,
causing the grass to grow?
   *(Pause)*

Who is father to the rain?
Who is mother to the dew?
Who has given birth to frost,
or carried ice within her womb?"   *(Job 38:22-30)*
   *(Pause)*

**LEADER**  O the depth
of the riches
and the wisdom
and the knowledge of God!
How incomprehensible Her judgements!
How mysterious Her ways!

**ALL**  Who can know the mind of God?
Who could ever be Her counselor?

## SILENT PRAYER

**READER**  "Can you restrain the Pleiades
or loose Orion's bonds?
Season after season,
can you guide the morning star?
   *(Pause)*

Have you grasped the laws
of the heavens?
Can you make them rule the earth?
Can your voice carry
up to the clouds?
Who will answer when you call?
   *(Pause)*

Does the hawk take wing
because of you,
the eagle soar
at your command?
How can you justify yourself?
Is your arm as strong as mine?"
*(Job 38:31-38; 39:26; 40:8-9)*
   *(Pause)*

**LEADER**  O the depth
of the riches
and the wisdom
and the knowledge of God!
How incomprehensible Her judgements!
How mysterious Her ways!

**ALL**  Who can know the mind of God?
Who could ever be Her counselor?

## SILENT PRAYER

## REFLECTION / SHARING

*Sit in a comfortable silence and reflect on the Mystery that is God.*

(Silent Reflection)

*Call to mind one compelling way in which the Mystery has been revealed to you in your life, and yet still remains a Mystery.*

(Silent Reflection)

*Share with one another a way in which God-as-mystery has been made manifest to you. Speak from your heart. If the assembly is small enough, remain together, otherwise share in groups of three.*

**ALL SING**    "Mystery" (See page 216.)

## PRAYER REFLECTION

| | |
|---|---|
| **LEADER** | I am: |
| **ALL** | Alpha. |
| **LEADER** | I am: |
| **ALL** | Omega. |
| **LEADER** | I am: |
| **ALL** | the Beginning. |
| **LEADER** | I am: |
| **ALL** | the End. |
| **LEADER** | I am: |
| **ALL** | the Way. |
| **LEADER** | I am: |
| **ALL** | the Truth. |
| **LEADER** | I am: |
| **ALL** | Everlasting Life. |
| **LEADER** | I am: |
| **ALL** | the Gate. |
| **LEADER** | I am: |
| **ALL** | the Vine. |
| **LEADER** | I am: |
| **ALL** | Living Water. |
| **LEADER** | I am: |
| **ALL** | the Bread of Life. |
| **LEADER** | I am: |
| **ALL** | the Light of the World. |
| **LEADER** | I am: |
| **ALL** | Who was. |
| **LEADER** | I am: |
| **ALL** | Who will be. |

| | |
|---|---|
| **LEADER** | I am |
| **ALL** | Who I am. |
| **LEADER** | I am for you |
| **ALL** | Who I will be for you. |
| **LEADER** | I am: |
| **ALL** | Alpha. |
| **LEADER** | I am: |
| **ALL** | Omega. |
| **LEADER** | I am: |
| **ALL** | the Beginning. |
| **LEADER** | I am: |
| **ALL** | the End. |
| **LEADER** | I am the rays of the rising sun, |
| **ALL** | snow on the Mountains of the Moon, |
| **LEADER** | the far-flung canopy of stars, |
| **ALL** | the shadows of late afternoon. |
| **LEADER** | I am the Wisdom of the sage. |
| **ALL** | I am the Refuge of all who weep. |
| **LEADER** | I am the Mother of all who live. |
| **ALL** | I am the Promises I keep. |
| **LEADER** | I am the One who sits with sorrow. |
| **ALL** | I am the One who feels your pain. |
| **LEADER** | I am the Hope of your tomorrow. |
| **ALL** | I am the One who will remain. |
| **LEADER** | With Me, |
| **ALL** | you will know compassion. |
| **LEADER** | Through Me, |
| **ALL** | you will comprehend. |
| **LEADER** | In Me, |
| **ALL** | you will not falter. |
| **ALL** | I am within you, without end. |

## BENEDICTION

| | |
|---|---|
| **LEADER** | May you (we) live the Mystery, and love the Mystery, and be caught up and held secure in the Mystery, whose wisdom exceeds all human knowledge, whose ways surpass all understanding, whose blessing fulfills our every hope, now and forever. |
| **ALL** | Amen. |

# LIBERATION RITUALS

*Freeing the Feminine in Worship*

**The Word
within
the biblical word
is the source
of womanly
wisdom.**

# THE VISIT

**LEADER**    Let us enter into silence.

## SILENT PRAYER

**LEADER**    Visit, O Holy Spirit,
this dedicated company
assembled for prayer and praise.
Through You, may we experience
the wisdom of God's Word
and the power of God's presence,
this day and forever.

**ALL**    Amen.

**READER**    The angel said to Mary:
"The Holy Spirit will come upon you,
and the power of the Most High
will overshadow you,
and the child to be born of you
will be called the Child of God." *(Lk 1:35)*

**LEADER**    May the One who comes,
come again in us.

**ALL**    May the One who comes
become in us
love-made-visible to all. Amen.

**VOICE ONE**    She was visited by an angel,
with the name of a man,
and was asked to do something

|  |  |
|---|---|
|  | no one on earth<br>had ever done before. |
| **ALL** | Hail, Mary!<br>Woman among women,<br>heroine of all the earth. |
| **VOICE ONE** | She was filled with the Holy Spirit:<br>bone of her bone,<br>flesh of her flesh,<br>blood of her blood,<br>God with us,<br>God among us<br>in a very womanly way. |
| **ALL** | Hail, Mary!<br>Woman among women,<br>heroine of all the earth. |
| **VOICE ONE** | Transformation,<br>Transubstantiation,<br>woman's whole being,<br>body and blood,<br>soul and spirit,<br>is living Eucharist!<br>Give thanks to God,<br>and praise,<br>all women,<br>all our days. |
| **ALL** | Hail, Mary!<br>Woman among women,<br>heroine of all the earth. |
| **VOICE ONE** | God always favors<br>the favorless,<br>those cast aside,<br>a burden to society<br>or of little consequence.<br>A woman,<br>least among least,<br>chosen by God<br>to make God present:<br>our first New Testament priest. |
| **ALL** | Hail, Mary!<br>Woman among women,<br>heroine of all the earth. |
| **READER** | "And behold, your kinswoman Elizabeth<br>in her old age<br>has also conceived a child;<br>this is the sixth month with her<br>who was barren.<br>Nothing is impossible with God!"<br>And Mary said, |

"I am completely open.
Mold me according to Your word." *(Lk 1:36-37)*

## SILENT REFLECTION

**READER**  In those days,
Mary arose and went with haste
into the hill country,
to a city of Judah,
to the house of Zechariah,
to be with Elizabeth.
When Elizabeth heard Mary's greeting,
her baby leaped in her womb,
and the old woman,
filled with the Holy Spirit,
shouted: "Blessed are you among women!
Blessed is the child of your womb!" *(Lk 1:39-42)*

**VOICE ONE**  And Mary sang a song of praise,
jubilant praise,
prophetic praise,
to the glory of her God.

**ALL SING**  "Magnificat" (See page 219.)

*After each of the following passages, as time permits, invite those present to reflect and respond with the promptings of their own hearts.*

**VOICE TWO**  An angel, in the guise of a man,
the same angel, Gabriel,
visited two women,
one old and one young,
with an invitation from God
to be part of, to experience,
something miraculous.
Both times
the messenger was male,
a masculine angel,
if you will.
Both times
the recipient of the message
and the miracle
was a woman.

## SHARED REFLECTION

**VOICE TWO**  Both times
a miracle happened
because a woman believed.
Both times
a woman's faith
had to withstand
man's incredulity.

Zechariah said, "That's absurd!"
when the angel Gabriel
took the time
to explain the case to him.
"How shall this be, for I am an old man,
and my wife is advanced in years?" *(Lk 1:18)*
I think Luke wrote it up this way
to soften the blow,
man to man,
because the man made a fool of himself
in acting like a man,
in doubting like a man.
Luke made him sound like Mary's naive
"How shall this be, for I have no husband?" *(Lk 1:34)*
But Zechariah, experienced,
truly doubted,
while Mary, innocent,
was appropriately confused.
And God punished Zechariah,
silenced his preaching,
silenced his teaching,
until he could come to his senses
when face to face with the facts.
Elizabeth probably clutched her belly
and sang
and danced
and laughed!

Joseph?
He wrestled with the consequences,
then dutifully obeyed.
Subordinate to Mary, a woman,
he supported her calling,
her ministry,
trusting her, a woman
in a male-centered society,
to set new precedents,
because she was of God.
Blessed be this gentle man!
Blessed be Mary,
visited by grace.
Blessed be her visit
to another woman
who had also known disgrace.

## SHARED REFLECTION

VOICE TWO   Luke records the visit.
Elizabeth is six months pregnant
when Mary hears the news.
The younger, also pregnant,
sets out at once for her cousin's home
and remains three months with her.

At the end of nine months,
Mary leaves,
and Elizabeth delivers a son,
according to the Gospel of Luke.
Do you really believe that's true?
Would you, as a woman,
would any woman
stay three months with an old, old relative
experiencing her first pregnancy,
then leave before the birth,
leave moments before the birth?
That isn't the way it is done,
in the village,
in the extended family,
among women,
then or now.
Her concern for the aged Elizabeth,
her curiosity, if nothing else,
kept Mary among the kinsfolk
who remained and rejoiced with her.
That may not be what the text says,
but my heart says it is so.
Does Luke
in retrospect
balk at the Messiah's mother
engaged in midwifery,
and the Christ
present
preparing the way
for the birth of the one destined
to prepare the way for him?
It may be disconcerting
and hierarchically incorrect,
but women, at ease with paradox,
prefer a theology
that follows the facts
of life and love and service.
Blessed be our God forever!

## SHARED REFLECTION

**VOICE TWO**    Isn't it ironic?
How many rights
have been denied to women—
human rights,
religious rites—
simply because we are women
and because Christ was a man?
Sojourner Truth
spoke the truth in 1852:
"Where did your Christ come from?
From God and a woman!
Man had nothing to do with Him!"

God was born of woman.
"And ain't I a woman?"
she said.
And aren't we women too?

## SHARED REFLECTION

## PRAYER OF THE COMMUNITY

**INDIVIDUALS** *Pray spontaneously for the needs of our world, particularly for the needs of women. After each petition All respond: "Visit us, Holy Spirit!"*

**ALL**　　　　 Visit us, Holy Spirit!

**LEADER**　　 Loving God, maternal God,
You are indeed full of surprises,
You are always bringing to birth.
You visited Mary
and made of her
a model for all women.
Mary visited Elizabeth
and, touched by grace,
left us with
a legacy of praise,
a hint of future miracles,
experience of God's ways:
the lowly are uplifted,
the powerful overthrown,
the hungry offered sustenance,
the resources of the wealthy given
to the underprivileged class.
Thank You, God of people,
for revealing Your feminine face.
Visit us now, and always,
with Your renewing grace.
For this we pray.

**ALL**　　　　 Amen.

**ALL SING**　 "The Visit" (See page 221.)

## BENEDICTION

**LEADER**　　 May the God of Eve and her offspring,
the God of Sarah, Rebecca, and Rachel,
the God of Mary and all who love her,
bless you (us), protect you (us), and grant you (us) peace,
now and forever.

**ALL**　　　　 Amen.

# WORD-MADE-FLESH

**LEADER**
The Word is made flesh
and lives with us.
Let us give thanks and praise!

**ALL SING**

Thank You, God, for the gift of birth, for
love made flesh to re - fresh the earth. For life and strength and
length of days, we give You thanks and praise.

Miriam Therese Winter

**LEADER**      Let us pray:

## SILENT PRAYER

**LEADER**      Inhabit our hearts,
God of history,
as You once inhabited
human flesh.
Be here among us
with all of Your wisdom,
all of Your power,
all of Your mercy,
all of Your love,
that we might learn
to be like God
from our God who came
to be like us.
Holy are You.
Holy are we
who are one with You forever.

**ALL**      Amen.

**READER**      In the beginning
before the mountains had been shaped,
before the hills,
before the beginning of the earth:
In the beginning,
before the birdsong
or the breath of life
lifted its gift
to the warmth of the sun:
In the beginning
was the Word
and the Word was with God
when God established the heavens,
when God drew a circle on the face of the deep,
when God marked out the foundations of the earth,
the Word was with God,
and the Word was God.
The Word was Power,
empowering all,
and the Word was Light,
enlightening all,
and the Word was Love,
loving all.
And the Word became flesh
and lived with us;
Ultimate Truth,
Source of Grace,
made of our world
a holy place,
as it was in the beginning,
is now,

and shall be
always and forever.
*(Based on Gen 1; Jn 1:1-14; Prov 8:22-31)*

# CREED

**VOICE ONE**   We believe that in the beginning was the Word,
that the Word was with God,
that the Word was God;
that through the Word all things began;
through an outpouring of love
God created the heavens and the earth.

**ALL SING**

We be - lieve in the Word - made - flesh, God's pres - ence in the world.

*(or)*

We be - lieve in the Word - made - flesh, God's pres - ence in the world.

Miriam Therese Winter
Copyright © Medical Mission Sisters, 1976

**VOICE ONE**   We believe that God touched earth,
and in a rush of tenderness
fashioned man and woman,
formed them in God's image,
loving them
as a mother loves her child.

**ALL SING**   We believe in the Word-made-flesh,
God's presence in the world.

**VOICE ONE**   We believe that God walked with us
from the beginning,
in the cool of the evening
and the heat of the day,
gifted us with freedom to achieve
and to fail,
liberated us whenever our bondage
became more than we could bear.

**ALL SING**   We believe in the Word-made-flesh,
God's presence in the world.

**VOICE ONE**   We believe that after a long period of waiting,
the God of history in fact became flesh
to share our human condition:
the salt of our tears,

the thrust of our dreams,
the intensity of our loves.
We believe that God came,
comes,
will come again,
enlightening our darkness,
satisfying our hungers,
forgiving our sins.

**ALL SING**    We believe in the Word-made-flesh,
God's presence in the world.

**VOICE ONE**    We believe that God chose woman
to be in partnership with God,
that God chooses woman
again and again
to live and love as God:
to give birth to deeper values,
to give flesh to the Gospel,
to touch, to heal, to listen, to care,
to feed the multitudes
with the daily bread of life.

**ALL SING**    We believe in the Word-made-flesh,
God's presence in the world.

**VOICE ONE**    We believe the Word is with us now
and will be until the end of time,
visibly present
wherever there are people
who live and love as God.
We believe that there is hope for tomorrow
despite discouragements today.
For with Sarah, Rebecca, and Rachel,
with all the prophetic women and saints,
we cling to the promise
of a new world order,
and we believe
that promise is being fulfilled.

**ALL SING**    We believe in the Word-made-flesh,
God's presence in the world.

## SILENT PRAYER

**LEADER**    If the Word is to take flesh again,
the Word must be made welcome,
the Word must be received
and made visible
in us.

**VOICE TWO**    In the beginning
again
the Word
at work within

without being heard;
through the din
of distraction
the fullness of power
is stifled;
kerygma,
kairos,
the hour of grace
passes
without a trace,
except in the bowels
of the spirit
is stirred
an unutterable ache
to be one
with the Word.

## SILENT PRAYER

**LEADER**     The Word continues
to pursue our hearts.
For those times that we can
truly say:
I am in the Word,
and the Word is in me,
let us give thanks and praise.

**ALL SING**     "Thank You, God" (See page 223.)

## SILENT PRAYER

**READER**     The Word was made flesh
and lived among us,
full of grace and truth.   *(Jn 1:14)*
     *(Pause, then repeat the statement.)*

**VOICE THREE**
Flesh of our flesh,
bone of our bone:
God was born of woman alone,
nursed at her breast,
clung to her knee,
shared thirty full years of silence
with her,
and broke it
only for three.
     *(Pause)*

Women have much in common
with God,
secrets that only women share,
of the womb,
of the heart,
of bringing to birth

and sustaining life
and becoming aware,
a giving,
forgiving,
nurturing role,
intent on making whoever is broken
whole.
   *(Pause)*

Is that why men are so afraid?
Afraid to share
prestige or power,
afraid to acknowledge
woman's worth,
because the power
of giving birth
is life,
meaning,
ultimate truth,
and she carries it all
within her?
For making flesh
is the moment when
woman and God
take charge again.
Is that why man
shuts woman out
from all other avenues of growth,
disdains her gifts,
fears her touch,
because she already has
too much?
   *(Pause)*

Word-made-flesh:
God understands
a woman's world
and the work of her hands:
the stress of feeding a multitude
with too many mouths
and too little food;
a wedding feast and no more wine:
"Woman, is that a concern
of mine?"
"Well, yes," she said,
and the vintage flowed;
and sometime later,
when a cup was passed
at a Supper
that would be the last,
a promise was made
so there would always be

enough for all:
Remember me
when you eat
and drink
in company.
   *(Pause)*

Thus says God:
I will be heard!
Make flesh
of my every word:
give peace, justice, liberty
visible reality;
feed the hungry,
don't just meet
and plan
what they will one day eat.
Shelter the homeless,
help the poor,
the destitute,
the insecure.
Preach with your hands,
wear out your shoes:
words alone are not Good News.
   *(Pause)*

Perhaps it is the time
again
for women of wisdom
to counsel men:
waging wars,
stating facts
are not the ways
a woman acts:
in giving life,
in meeting needs,
a woman feels,
a woman feeds;
once in the womb,
once in the crèche,
then again and again
the Word takes flesh.

## SILENT PRAYER

**LEADER**     Let us reflect together
on woman's unique capacity
to make flesh:
not only in her own womb,
but in the wider womb of the world.
Men tend to deal in abstractions;
a woman's world is concrete.

Men tend to see things one at a time.
To women, life is all of a piece,
wholistic, inclusive, interrelated.
Women translate theory into practice
and do it quite naturally.
Reflect for a moment on this:
*conceptual* means having to do with ideas,
with concepts, with the abstract;
*conception* has to do with birth,
the beginning of new life;
one can either conceive of an idea,
or one can conceive a child.
Women are comfortable with children,
and equally comfortable with ideas.
Concepts are a lot like children:
they need to be given life,
to be enfleshed,
to be made real.
Words are nothing more than words
until they are made real.
Jesus came as Word-made-flesh,
came to woman
as Word-made-flesh,
so that all God's words
might be real.

## SILENT REFLECTION

*How does this unique capacity of woman to "make flesh" contribute to our understanding of the Gospel of Jesus?*

*Choose a particular Gospel ethic, or value, or message, or theme. How might you give flesh to this during the coming year?*

## SHARED REFLECTION

*Share with one another the fruit of your reflection, and listen with your heart.*

## PRAYER OF THE COMMUNITY

*To each spontaneous, individual prayer, All respond: "Word-made-flesh, have mercy!"*

**LEADER**    In our own words now,
let us pray for the world
and for all who suffer
from any need.

**ALL**    Word-made-flesh, have mercy!

**LEADER**    We thank You
and praise You,
Word-made-flesh,

for Your presence here
in our midst,
for making our world
a hallowed place,
for giving a human touch
to grace.
Be with us now
as we try to give flesh
and meaning
to Your Gospel.
Help us translate words
into deeds
that reach to the depth
of human needs,
following Your example,
God of compassion,
God of people.

**ALL**      Amen.

**ALL SING**    "We Are the Word" (See page 225.)

## BENEDICTION

**LEADER**    May the blessing of the Holy One who gives us life,
the blessing of the Human One who redeems our life,
the blessing of the Spirit who enriches our life,
be with us all.

**ALL**      Amen.

# EPIPHANY

| | |
|---|---|
| **LEADER** | What do you seek<br>from this celebration? |
| **ALL** | Our hearts seek<br>a revelation. |
| **LEADER** | Pray, then,<br>that what has been concealed<br>from the wise<br>this day<br>might be revealed. |

## SILENT PRAYER

| | |
|---|---|
| **LEADER** | Light of the world,<br>we bow before You<br>in awe and adoration.<br>Bless us<br>and our simple faith<br>seeking understanding.<br>Epiphany means<br>manifestation,<br>lifting the veil,<br>revelation.<br>Reveal to us then<br>what we need to know<br>to love You,<br>and serve You,<br>and keep Your word<br>with fidelity and truth, |

|         | courage and hope,<br>this day and always. |
|---------|---|
| **ALL** | Amen. |
| **LEADER** | Prepare your hearts to hear God's word,<br>as recorded in Matthew's account of the Gospel,<br>and consider the following questions<br>as you listen to the text. |
|         | Who are the cast of characters,<br>and what is their role in the script? |
|         | Is anything said about women,<br>and what does the story suggest<br>about the lives and the lifestyles of men? |
| **READER** | After Jesus had been born<br>in Bethlehem<br>in Judea<br>in the days of Herod the king,<br>wise men came<br>to Jerusalem<br>from the East,<br>inquiring:<br>"Where is the one born<br>king of the Jews?<br>We have seen his star<br>and have come to pay homage."<br>Herod heard<br>and was disturbed,<br>and all of Jerusalem with him.<br>Assembling some scribes<br>and priests of the people,<br>he inquired of them<br>where the Christ would be born.<br>"In Bethlehem of Judea,<br>as the prophet foretold,<br>'And you, O Bethlehem,<br>in the land of Judah,<br>are by no means least<br>among the leaders of Judah:<br>from you will come a leader<br>to govern Israel.' "<br>Herod summoned the wise men<br>secretly<br>to ascertain<br>when the star had appeared,<br>then sent them on, saying,<br>"Search for the child,<br>and when you have found him,<br>let me know,<br>so that I too may pay homage."<br>Having heard the king, |

they went their way,
following the star
until it came to rest;
and they entered the house
and saw the child
with Mary his mother,
and falling to their knees,
they paid him homage,
then opened their treasures
and offered him gifts
of gold
and frankincense
and myrrh.
They were warned in a dream
to avoid Herod,
and returned to their country
by a different way.
Then an angel appeared to Joseph
in a dream,
saying, "Rise,
take the child
and his mother
and flee,
for Herod intends
to destroy him."
So he took the child
and his mother
and fled into Egypt.
When Herod realized
the wise men were gone
and he had been tricked,
he was livid with rage
and had all the male children
under two years of age
in Bethlehem
and the surrounding region
slaughtered,
fulfilling the words of Jeremiah
the prophet:
"A voice was heard in Ramah, wailing;
Rachel weeping for her children,
refusing to be comforted,
because they were no more."
After Herod's death,
the angel of God
appeared in a dream
to Joseph in Egypt, saying,
"Rise, take the child
and his mother
and return to Israel,
for those who would kill the child
are dead."

So he rose
and took the child
and his mother
and returned to Israel.
On learning that Archelaus
had succeeded Herod his father
as ruler of Judea,
Joseph was afraid to go there.
He was warned in a dream,
and they settled in Galilee
in a town called Nazareth,
so the words of the prophet
might be fulfilled,
"He shall be called a Nazarene." *(Mt 2:1-23)*

LEADER  Let us reflect quietly now
on this story and the questions,
before sharing what we think and feel.
The questions again are:
who are the cast of characters,
and what is their role in the script?
Is anything said about women,
and what does the story suggest
about the lives and the lifestyles of men?

## SILENT REFLECTION

## SHARED REFLECTION

*Share your reflections about the characters in the story and their respective roles. What do you think is implied in the references to women? What information is communicated in the references to men?*

*Here are additional questions for reflection and discussion:*

*What do you think is the point of the story?*

*How do you feel about the story and its traditional interpretation?*

*Whether the story is fact or fiction, how would you as a woman retell the story or reshape its interpretation?*

LEADER  Let us listen now
to a final reflection
on the traditional Epiphany text.

VOICE  The men in the story,
and there are many,
have typical masculine roles,
positions of power,
positions of prestige,
with titles
or descriptive phrases
bound to impress
and all the trappings appropriate to

the culturally privileged class:
wise men
who travel abroad
with their cumulative wealth,
Herod the king
who dominates
and oppresses the weak,
priests and scribes
who know it all,
prophets
such as Jeremiah
and others
cited canonically,
and Archelaus
who also ruled.
Even Joseph is seen
through filtered eyes
as head of the house,
the one in charge
who makes the decisions,
who gets the message
straight from the heavenly realm.
The women—
there are only two—
are subordinate
or invisible:
one is silent,
and the other weeps.
Power sees
what it wants to see.
The wise men sought
the king of the Jews
and laid their agenda
on a little child,
worshiped him,
showered him
with a wealth of gifts,
missed the whole point
of who he was
and why he was:
no wonder Mary was silent,
no wonder Rachel wept.
The wise men left
a little less wise
than when they had arrived.
So it is with those
conditioned by power
and privilege
and ease.
Institutionalized pride
will eventually fall.
May God have mercy
on us all.

## SILENT PRAYER

**LEADER**     What have you found
in this celebration?

**ALL**     Our hearts have found
a revelation.

**LEADER**     We give thanks
and we praise the Holy Spirit:
God's revealed word
is ever revealing;
what has been hidden
from the learned and wise
is made known to the simple of heart.
We give thanks for a rich tradition
of new and needed meaning
coming forth from the word of God.
We remain one in spirit
with this our tradition,
as we affirm our faith
through an apostolic creed.

**ALL**     We believe in God,
All-merciful, Almighty,
Maker of heaven and earth,
and in Jesus the Christ,
the Child of God,
conceived by the Holy Spirit,
born of the Virgin Mary,
who suffered under Pontius Pilate,
was crucified, died,
and was buried.
After three days in the tomb,
Jesus rose from the dead,
ascended into heaven,
and reigns forever
as the right hand of God,
who will come again to judge
the living and the dead.
We believe in the Holy Spirit,
the universal Church,
the communion of saints,
the forgiveness of sins,
the resurrection of the body,
and life everlasting. Amen.

## BENEDICTION

**LEADER**     May you (we) be blessed with a wealth of wisdom.
May you (we) worship as God intends.
May the gifts that you (we) give
be the gifts you (we) receive:

goodness and mercy,
generosity and peace,
now and forever.

**ALL**      Amen.

**SONG**    "Hear God's Word" (See page 227.)

# WHY DO YOU WEEP?

*Each of the three sections introduced by the lament can be treated as a separate celebration, along with the closing prayer and song. Consider a Lenten series on the theme "Why Do You Weep?" using these selections as a basis on which to build and expand your own community prayer and shared reflection.*

## FIRST LAMENT

**VOICE**  All who pass by,
look and see:
is there any sorrow like my sorrow?  *(Lam 1:12)*

## HANNAH'S STORY

**CHORUS**  Hannah, why do you weep?
And why is your heart sad?

**READER**  There was a certain man
of the hill country of Ephraim,
whose name was Elkanah,
the son of Jeroham,
son of Elihu,
son of Tohu,
son of Zuph,
an Ephraimite.

**CHORUS**  Hannah, why do you weep?
And why is your heart sad?

**READER**  Elkanah had two wives.
The name of the one was Hannah,
and the name of the other,
Peninnah.

| | |
|---|---|
| **CHORUS** | Hannah, why do you weep?<br>And why is your heart sad? |
| **READER** | Peninnah had children.<br>Hannah had none.<br>On the day when Elkanah sacrificed,<br>he gave portions to Peninnah<br>and to all her sons and daughters;<br>and although he loved Hannah,<br>he gave her only one portion,<br>because Yahweh had closed her womb. |
| **CHORUS** | Hannah, why do you weep?<br>And why is your heart sad? |
| **READER** | Her rival used to provoke her sorely,<br>to irritate her,<br>because Yahweh had closed her womb.<br>And so it went on,<br>year after year.<br>And Elkanah, her husband,<br>said to her: |
| **CHORUS** | "Hannah, why do you weep?<br>And why is your heart sad?" |
| **READER** | Hannah, deeply distressed,<br>prayed to God in the temple,<br>weeping bitterly. |
| **CHORUS** | Hannah, why do you weep?<br>And why is your heart sad? |
| **READER** | She made a vow to God, saying,<br>"If You will remember me,<br>if You will look upon my affliction,<br>if You will give Your maidservant a son,<br>I will give the child back to You<br>all the days of his life." |
| **CHORUS** | Hannah, why do you weep?<br>And why is your heart sad? |
| **READER** | Eli the priest,<br>observing her,<br>took her to be a drunk<br>and said:<br>"Put away your wine!" |
| **CHORUS** | Hannah, why do you weep?<br>And why is your heart sad? |
| **READER** | "Neither wine nor strong drink<br>have I drunk.<br>I have poured out my soul<br>before my God. |

|  |  |
|---|---|
|  | I have prayed, not with words, but with my heart, speaking out of my vexation and my great anxiety." |
| **CHORUS** | Hannah, why do you weep? And why is your heart sad? |
| **READER** | "Go in peace," Eli replied, "and may God grant your desire." So Hannah conceived and bore a son, and when he was weaned, she went up to Shiloh, to Eli the priest, and gave the child back to God. |
| **CHORUS** | Hannah, why do you weep? And why is your heart sad? |
| **READER** | "My heart exults in God, my whole being is exalted. There is none holy as Yahweh, in whose power I rejoice. For the bows of the mighty are broken, and the weak are girded with strength. Those who were full now work for their bread, and the famished no longer hunger. Yahweh raises the poor from the dust and the needy out of the ashes, giving them places of honor, for the humble are lifted up. The one who was barren has borne a child, but the mother of many is desolate. My heart exults in God, my whole being is exalted. Blessed be God forever!" *(1 Sam 1; 2:1-10)* |

# REFLECTION / SHARING

*Imagine you are Hannah. Reflect on her life, which was typical of the lives of the women of her time. Then tell us, Hannah, why do you weep? Allow sufficient time for an unhurried group commentary on Hannah's story.*

*(If you are ending the prayer service after the group sharing, move to the closing prayer and song beginning on page 97.)*

*(If you are ending the prayer service after the group sharing, move to the closing prayer and song beginning on page 97.)*

## SECOND LAMENT

|  |  |
|---|---|
| **VOICE** | All who pass by, look and see: is there any sorrow like my sorrow? |

| | |
|---|---|
| **READER** | There followed a great multitude of people, and of women who wept and lamented. But Jesus turned to them and said: "Daughters of Jerusalem, do not weep for me, but weep for yourselves and for your children." *(Lk 23:27-28)* |
| **VOICE** | Daughters, do not weep for me, but weep for yourselves and for your children. |
| **SIDE ONE** | For the girl child in a man's world, |
| **SIDE TWO** | for women who did not count the cost, |
| **SIDE ONE** | when dreams had to be forfeited, |
| **SIDE TWO** | and opportunities were lost. |
| **VOICE** | Daughters, do not weep for me, but weep for yourselves and for your children. |
| **SIDE ONE** | Weep for the battered and abused. |
| **SIDE TWO** | Weep for the broken and oppressed. |
| **SIDE ONE** | Weep for the women who have been used. |
| **SIDE TWO** | Then weep some more for all the rest. |
| **VOICE** | Daughters, do not weep for me, but weep for yourselves and for your children. |
| **SIDE ONE** | Weep for the girl in her mother's womb. |
| **SIDE TWO** | Weep for the gemstone in the rough, |
| **SIDE ONE** | who from the cradle to the tomb |
| **SIDE TWO** | will never be quite good enough. |
| **VOICE** | Daughters, do not weep for me, but weep for yourselves and for your children. |

## SILENT PRAYER

| | |
|---|---|
| **READER** | Mary stood weeping outside the tomb. Weeping, she stooped to look into the tomb and saw two angels sitting there where the body of Jesus had been. They said to her, "Woman, why do you weep?" "Because they have taken my Lord away, and I know not where to find him." She turned and saw Jesus standing there, |

but she did not know who he was.
Jesus said, "Woman, why do you weep?
Who are you looking for?"
"Sir, if you have taken my Lord away,
tell me where I can find him."  *(Jn 20:11-15)*

## SILENT PRAYER

**VOICE**  Woman, why do you weep?

**ALL**  They have taken away my confidence,
and I know not where to find it.

**VOICE**  Woman, why do you weep?

**ALL**  They have taken away my identity,
and I know not where to find it.

**VOICE**  Woman, why do you weep?

**ALL**  They have taken away my Deity,
and I know not where to find Her.

## REFLECTION / SHARING

*Reflect quietly for several minutes on your own personal response to the following question, addressed directly to you: Woman, why do you weep? Then gather in small groups, or remain together, if the setting and size is conducive, and share your response with one another.*

*(If you are ending the prayer service after the group sharing, move to the closing prayer and song beginning on page 97.)*

*(If you are ending the prayer service after the group sharing, move to the closing prayer and song beginning on page 97.)*

### THIRD LAMENT

**VOICE**  All who pass by,
look and see:
is there any sorrow like my sorrow?

**READER**  Herod,
realizing he had been tricked
by the sages,
in a fit of rage
ordered all male children
under two years of age
throughout his territory
killed.
The prophecy of Jeremiah
was thereby fulfilled:
"A voice was heard in Ramah, wailing;
Rachel weeping for her children,
refusing to be comforted,
because they were no more."  *(Mt 2:16-18; Jer 31:15)*

| | |
|---|---|
| **VOICE** | A voice is heard in Ramah, wailing; Rachel weeping for her children, refusing to be comforted, because they are no more. |
| **CHORUS** | Rachel weeping... |
| **VOICE** | violated... excluded... harassed... ignored... |
| **CHORUS** | Rachel weeping... |
| **VOICE** | raped... exploited... discriminated against... abused... |
| **CHORUS** | Rachel weeping... |
| **VOICE** | patronized... passed over... invisible... underpaid... |
| **CHORUS** | Rachel weeping for her children... |
| **VOICE** | trapped in a sexist society in a patriarchal world... |
| **CHORUS** | Rachel weeping for her children... |
| **VOICE** | because gender determines choices and stereotypes prevail... |
| **CHORUS** | Rachel weeping for her children... |
| **VOICE** | the ones who "hold up half the sky" and nobody seems to care... |
| **CHORUS** | Rachel weeping for her children, refusing to be comforted, because they are no more. |
| **VOICE** | They died of hunger... they succumbed to disease... |
| **CHORUS** | Rachel weeping for her children, refusing to be comforted, because they are no more. |
| **VOICE** | They were victims of genocide... expendable... |
| **CHORUS** | Rachel weeping for her children, refusing to be comforted, because they are no more. |
| **VOICE** | Her sons died in the fields and at the fronts of countless, senseless wars... |

| CHORUS | Rachel weeping for her children,<br>refusing to be comforted,<br>because they are no more. |
|---|---|
| VOICE | They killed one another ruthlessly,<br>to quench their thirst for power... |
| CHORUS | Rachel weeping for her children,<br>refusing to be comforted,<br>because they are no more. |
| VOICE | Her daughters were disposed of, quietly,<br>because boy babies were preferred... |
| CHORUS | Rachel weeping for her children,<br>refusing to be comforted,<br>because they are no more. |

## SILENT PRAYER

## REFLECTION / SHARING

*Spend some time exploring together the countless ways we destroy one
another: physically, psychologically, spiritually, culturally. Reflect on what
this destructive orientation does to woman's maternal spirit.*

## CLOSING PRAYER

| SIDE ONE | Deliver us from all the oppression<br>practiced under the sun. |
|---|---|
| SIDE TWO | Dry the tears of the oppressed,<br>and comfort every one. |
| SIDE ONE | God has heard the sound of our weeping.<br>Oppressive ones, beware! |
| SIDE TWO | God has heard our supplication.<br>God accepts our prayer. |
| SIDE ONE | Our weeping at the end of day<br>is turned to joy at dawn, |
| SIDE TWO | even though our woman-pain<br>is seldom ever gone. |
| SIDE ONE | Praise Shaddai, She will not let<br>injustices prevail. |
| SIDE TWO | Praise Shaddai, Her love endures,<br>Her favors never fail. |
| SIDE ONE | She turns our mourning into dancing,<br>silence into song. |
| SIDE TWO | She lifts us up and promises<br>redress will not be long. |
| SIDE ONE | Rejoice, She says, with those who rejoice,<br>and weep with those who mourn. |

| | |
|---|---|
| **SIDE TWO** | My daughters, She says, be comforted, your courage be reborn. |
| **SIDE ONE** | All of you who sow in tears, who struggle hard to cope, |
| **SIDE TWO** | your harvest will yield a hundredfold, you will reap the rewards of hope. |
| **SIDE ONE** | God will one day dry your tears, and death will be no more, |
| **SIDE TWO** | no poverty, discrimination, violence, or war. |
| **SIDE ONE** | Behold, new possibilities Her mercy will impart, |
| **SIDE TWO** | fulfilling all that you desire deep in your woman-heart. |

*(Based on verses from Eccles 4; Psalms 6, 30, 126; Rm 12; Rev 21)*

| | |
|---|---|
| **LEADER** | Jesus fixed his eyes on his disciples, and said: "Blessed are you that weep now, for one day you will laugh. Woe to you that laugh now, for you will mourn and weep." *(Lk 6:20-21,25)* "Truly, I say to you, you will weep and lament, while the world rejoices; you will be filled with sorrow, but your sorrow will turn into joy." *(Jn 16:20)* So it is with all who give birth to new hopes, new dreams, new visions, as we shape a new world order of equality and love, of justice and peace, forever and ever. |
| **ALL** | Amen. |
| **SONG** | "Coming Around Again" (See page 229.) |

# YOU SHALL BE MY WITNESSES

**LEADER**  You shall be my witnesses
through all the earth,
telling of all you have heard
and received,
for I arose and am with you,
and you have believed!

**ALL SING**

You shall be my wit-ness-es through all the earth,

tell-ing of all you have heard and re-ceived, for

I a-rose and am with you and you have be-lieved.

Miriam Therese Winter
Copyright © Medical Mission Sisters, 1987

**LEADER**       Let us pray:
                   *(pause for silent prayer)*

                 God of Good News,
                 God of surprises,
                 we come together to praise You
                 and to open ourselves wide
                 to Your intuitive touch.
                 Surrounded by a cloud of witnesses,
                 women of history,
                 named and unnamed,
                 known and unknown,
                 we drink deep of the wisdom
                 and fidelity
                 of the past,
                 the faith of our foremothers
                 who showed us how
                 to live what we believe.
                 When driven to doubt,
                 when close to despair,
                 may we still believe
                 in miracles
                 and witness courageously
                 to what might be
                 in Jesus the Christ.

**ALL**          Amen.

**READER**       It was the day of preparation,
                 and the sabbath was near at hand.
                 The women
                 who had come with Jesus
                 from Galilee
                 followed behind to the tomb
                 to see how his body was laid.
                 On the sabbath day
                 they rested.
                 But on the first day of the week,
                 early, at dawn,
                 they returned to the tomb
                 with the spices they had prepared.
                 The stone had been rolled away from the tomb,
                 and they could not find his body.
                 They were confused,
                 then terrified,
                 as two men clad in dazzling clothes
                 suddenly materialized,
                 saying:
                 "Why seek the living among the dead?
                 Remember, he told you
                 in Galilee
                 he would be crucified,
                 and on the third day

he would rise again.
He is not here.
He has risen."
They remembered his words,
and they left the tomb,
Mary of Magdala,
Joanna,
and Mary, the mother of James,
and the other women
who were with them,
and they reported to the apostles,
but their story sounded ridiculous,
and the apostles did not believe them.

*(Lk 23:54-55; 24:1-12)*

**SOLOIST SINGS** (See page 231.)
Women at the tomb,
weeping for the dead:
he is not here,
he has risen as he said.
They ran to tell those who were in authority.
The men dismissed the news as idle fantasy.

**ALL SING**    You shall be my witnesses
through all the earth,
telling of all you have heard and received,
for I arose and am with you,
and you have believed.

## SILENT PRAYER

**READER**    Very early
on the first day of the week,
while it was still dark,
Mary of Magdala came to the tomb.
Seeing the stone had been rolled aside,
she went running to Simon Peter
and to the disciple Jesus loved,
saying:
"They have taken the Lord
out of the tomb,
and we don't know where they have put him."
Both disciples ran to the tomb...
went inside...
and then went home again.
But Mary remained,
weeping.
When at last she stooped to look into the tomb,
she saw two angels sitting there
where the body of Jesus had been.
They said to her,
"Woman, why do you weep?"
"Because they have taken my Lord away

and I know not where to find him."
She turned and saw Jesus standing there,
but she did not know who he was.
Jesus said, "Woman, why do you weep?
Who are you looking for?"
Thinking he was the gardener, she said:
"Sir, if you have taken my Lord,
tell me where you have put him,
and I will take him away."
Jesus said, "Mary!"
She knew then who he was.
"Rabboni!" Master!
Eventually, Jesus said to her:
"Do not cling to me now.
I have not yet ascended.
Go and tell my followers
that I am ascending
to my God and yours."
So Mary of Magdala
went and told the disciples:
"I have seen the Lord."
And she told them all the things
that he had said to her. *(Jn 20:1-18)*

**SOLOIST SINGS** (See page 231.)
Magdalene at the tomb:
Whom do you seek?
Her eyes were opened
when she heard him speak.
His love for every woman shone upon his face.
The hopes of every age were held in their embrace.

**ALL SING**
You shall be my witnesses
through all the earth,
telling of all you have heard and received,
for I arose and am with you,
and you have believed.

## SILENT PRAYER

**READER**
Two disciples,
returning to their village,
Emmaus,
were joined by Jesus,
whom they did not recognize.
They discussed the events
of the preceding days,
how Jesus of Nazareth,
their hope for freeing Israel,
had been crucified.
And this also the disciples said:
"Moreover, some women of our company

astounded us.
Early in the morning
they were at the tomb,
and they could not find his body.
They said they had seen
a vision of angels
who said that he was alive.
Others of our company
went to the tomb
and saw it was just as the women had said,
but Jesus they did not see."
Then Jesus said to them:
"O foolish men!
So slow to believe
all that the prophets have spoken." *(Lk 24:22-25)*

**SOLOIST SINGS** (See page 231.)
Women at the tomb,
weeping for the dead:
He is not here,
he has risen as he said.
They ran to tell those who were in authority.
The men dismissed the news as idle fantasy.

**ALL SING**  You shall be my witnesses
through all the earth,
telling of all you have heard and received,
for I arose and am with you,
and you have believed.

## SILENT PRAYER

**ALL**  Forgive all
who are slow to believe
the witnesses of God.

**VOICE**  And Gabriel said to Zechariah:
"You will be silent,
unable to speak,
until the day these things come to pass,
because you did not believe." *(Lk 1:20)*

**ALL**  Forgive all
who are slow to believe
the witnesses of God.

**VOICE**  Jesus remained in Galilee,
because in Judea,
they were out to kill him.
Even his brothers
did not believe him. *(Jn 7:1,5)*

**ALL**  Forgive all
who are slow to believe
the witnesses of God.

| | |
|---|---|
| **VOICE** | Jesus said: "Prophets are not without honor except in their own country and in their own house." And he did not perform many miracles there, because of their unbelief.   *(Mt 13:57-58)* |
| **ALL** | Forgive all who are slow to believe the witnesses of God. |
| **VOICE** | Mary Magdalene, Joanna, Mary the mother of James, and all the women with them, told the apostles what they saw at the tomb, but they did not believe them.   *(Lk 24:10-11)* |
| **ALL** | Forgive all who are slow to believe the witnesses of God. |
| **VOICE** | Thomas was absent when Jesus appeared to the company in the upper room. The disciples told him: "We have seen the Lord!" But Thomas replied: "Unless I see in his hands the print of the nails, and put my finger on the mark of the nails, and place my hand on the wound in his side, I will not believe."   *(Jn 20:24-25)* |
| **ALL** | Forgive all who are slow to believe the witnesses of God. |

## SILENT PRAYER

| | |
|---|---|
| **LEADER** | To be a witness means coming to terms with stones and with believing. On Easter morning the women encountered a series of strange occurrences. The stone had been rolled from the door of the tomb. They saw things never seen before. But nobody would believe them. The stone was a seal, |

and the seal was broken,
and nobody would believe them.
The hearts of the leadership
had turned to stone.
No wonder they couldn't believe them.
The hearts of the women
were heavy as stone
because nobody would believe them.
Stone-cold.
Stone-deaf.
Stone-walled.
Words that are all too familiar.
Words that break our hearts.
Words well known to women,
who come up against immovable obstacles
at almost every turn.
Stones are the tests
of believers.
Do you believe the Living God
can roll any stone aside?

## REFLECTION / SHARING

*Reflect for a few minutes on what you feel is an obstacle to your full function-*
*ing as a woman in the Church or in society. What will it take to remove that*
*obstacle, to roll that stone aside?*

*After reflecting, share briefly in small groups, or all together, the particular*
*obstacle inhibiting you as a woman, and what you feel it would take to*
*liberate you.*

## SHARING THE VISION

*Spontaneously, in a single sentence, share what you envision for the Church*
*in terms of the witness and the ministry of women. Respond to each state-*
*ment with the following:*

**LEADER**    And Jesus said:

**ALL**    "You shall be my witnesses through all the earth."

## CLOSING PRAYER

**LEADER**    O Risen One,
you gave your Word,
saying:
"You will be given
power
when the Holy Spirit
comes upon you,
and you will be my witnesses
even to the ends of the earth."   *(Ac 1:8)*
Come, Spirit, now,
we pray:

| ALL | Come, Holy Spirit, |
| | empower us |
| | to witness to the ends of the earth. |

| LEADER | O Compassionate One, |
| | you gave your Promise, |
| | saying: |
| | "A new heart I will give you. |
| | A new spirit I will place within you. |
| | I will give you a heart of flesh |
| | and remove your heart of stone." *(Ez 36:26)* |
| | Come to us now, |
| | we pray: |

| ALL | Come, Holy Spirit, |
| | empower us |
| | to witness to the ends of the earth. |

| LEADER | O Comforting One, |
| | you gave us your secret, |
| | saying: |
| | "Let not your hearts be troubled. |
| | Believe in God. |
| | Believe in me. *(Jn 14:1)* |
| | Who comes to me, |
| | shall not hunger. |
| | Who believes in me, |
| | shall never thirst." *(Jn 6:35)* |
| | Come to us now, |
| | we pray: |

| ALL | Come, Holy Spirit, |
| | empower us |
| | to witness to the ends of the earth. |

## BENEDICTION

| LEADER | May the power of the Holy Spirit come upon you (us). |
| | May the wisdom of godly women encourage you (us). |
| | May the cloud of witnesses accompany you (us). |
| | And may you (we) witness to the ends of the earth. |

| ALL | Amen. |

| SONG | "You Shall Be My Witnesses" (See page 231.) |

# COME, SPIRIT

**ALL SING**

Come, Spir - it, come and be a new re - al - i - ty.___

___ Your touch is guar - an - tee of love a - live in me.

**Miriam Therese Winter**
Copyright © Medical Mission Sisters, 1982

| | |
|---|---|
| **SIDE ONE** | Come, Spirit: as light in darkness... |
| **SIDE TWO** | Come, Spirit: as rain in drought... |
| **SIDE ONE** | Come, Spirit: as warmth in winter... |
| **SIDE TWO** | Come, Spirit: and bail us out. |
| **ALL SING** | Come, Spirit, come and be a new reality. Your touch is guarantee of love alive in me. |
| **SIDE ONE** | Come: visit the unenlightened... |
| **SIDE TWO** | Come: slake our staggering thirst... |
| **SIDE ONE** | Come: establish the ways of justice... |
| **SIDE TWO** | Come: be with us through the worst. |

| | |
|---|---|
| **ALL SING** | Come, Spirit, come and be a new reality.<br>Your touch is guarantee of love alive in me. |
| **SIDE ONE** | Come, Spirit: as healing and wholeness... |
| **SIDE TWO** | Come, Spirit: as life-giving food... |
| **SIDE ONE** | Come, Spirit: as hope in oppression... |
| **SIDE TWO** | Come, Spirit: as all that is good. |
| **ALL SING** | Come, Spirit, come and be a new reality.<br>Your touch is guarantee of love alive in me. |
| **SIDE ONE** | Come: banish discrimination... |
| **SIDE TWO** | Come: wash its wounds away... |
| **SIDE ONE** | Come: break the bread of freedom... |
| **SIDE TWO** | Come: declare a holy day. |
| **ALL SING** | Come, Spirit, come and be a new reality.<br>Your touch is guarantee of love alive in me. |
| **SIDE ONE** | Come, Spirit: you are the victory... |
| **SIDE TWO** | Come, Spirit: you are the grace... |
| **ALL SAY** | Come, Spirit: you are the reason<br>this gathering is a holy place.<br>Come, Spirit, Come! |
| **ALL SING** | Come, Spirit, come and be a new reality.<br>Your touch is guarantee of love alive in me. |
| **LEADER** | Come, Spirit,<br>renew the hearts<br>of all who are gathered<br>for prayer and praise,<br>renew the structures<br>that order our lives,<br>renew the lifestyle<br>that structures our days,<br>renew the earth<br>with countless initiatives<br>for justice<br>and peace,<br>liberation<br>and life,<br>now and every day.<br>Amen. |
| **LEADER** | Let us listen to the Word of God.<br>Let us hear again how the Holy Spirit<br>took hold of the followers of Jesus<br>in the very early days of the newly emerging Church.<br>They were all of them gathered together,<br>apostles and disciples, women and men, |

in Jerusalem, in that upper room,
having recently watched the Risen Jesus
ascend to the Living God.

**READER**      From the Mount of Olives,
they returned to Jerusalem,
and went together to the upper room
where they were staying:
Peter and John,
James and Andrew,
Philip and Thomas,
Bartholomew and Matthew,
James son of Alphaeus,
Simon the Zealot,
and Jude son of James.
All these devoted themselves to prayer,
together with the women,
with Mary the mother of Jesus,
and with his brothers.
When the day of Pentecost came around,
they were all together there,
in that room,
when suddenly the sound
of a rushing wind
shook the house
where they were sitting,
and they saw
what seemed like
tongues of fire
hovering above
each one of them
and all were filled
with the Holy Spirit
and began to speak
in different tongues
in the power of the Spirit.
Hearing this sound,
a crowd assembled,
devout people
from every nation known on earth,
Parthians, Medes, and Elamites,
people from Mesopotamia,
from Judea and Cappadocia,
Pontus and Asia,
Phrygia and Pamphylia,
Egypt and the parts of Libya around Cyrene,
Jews and proselytes,
Cretans and Arabians
who were visiting from Rome.
All were amazed and astonished,
for all of them heard
their own language,

heard them preach
in their own language
the wonderful works of God.
They tried to laugh it off, saying:
"They drank too much new wine."
But Peter stood up
and, raising his voice,
contradicted them.
"We are not drunk,
as you suppose.
It is only the beginning
of the day.
These words of the prophet
have come to pass:

'In the days to come,
it is God who speaks,
I will pour out My Spirit
on all humankind.
Your sons and your daughters
shall prophesy.
The young shall see visions.
The old shall dream dreams.
Even on My slaves,
both women and men,
I will pour out My Spirit
in those days,
and they shall prophesy.' " *(Ac 1:12-14; 2:1-18)*

**READER**     This is the word of God.

**ALL**     Thanks be to God.

## SILENT PRAYER

**LEADER**     Those very first moments of the birth of the Church
were inclusive. We sense a comfortable equality
between women and men, as recorded in the Book of Acts.
Women were there in the upper room, praying fervently,
together with the men. Mary the mother of Jesus was
there. They were all together on the day of Pentecost.
All felt the force of the Spirit. All were touched
by tongues of fire. All began to speak in tongues.
All were accused by the crowd of being drunk, women
as well as men. The preaching of all was understood
by the crowd, the preaching of women as well as men.
Peter explained this phenomenon by referring to the
prophecy of Joel, showing how this moment had been
foretold, how on that day the power of the Spirit
would be felt by all, by women as well as men.
How does this match your own experience as a woman?
How does this description of the early Church compare
with your own Church experience?

## SHARED HOMILY

*After reflecting on what you have heard and listening attentively to what your own heart is saying, share your reflections on what the text is saying in relation to your own experience, or any insight the Spirit gives you. Be open to the Spirit speaking to and through this assembly.*

## CALLING ON THE SPIRIT

| ALL | | LEADER | |
|-----|-------|--------|---|
| Come! | | | Morning Star |
| Come! | | | Cool of evening |
| Come! | | | Dark night of the soul |
| Come! | | | Source of illumination |
| Come! | | | Essence of inspiration |
| Come! | | | Swift as a sudden shower |
| Come! | | | Sweet as a mountain spring |
| Come! | | | Borne on chariots of cloud |
| Come! | | | Riding the wings of the wind |
| Come! | | | Breath of God |
| Come! | | | Finger of God's right hand |
| Come! | | | Song of the universe |
| Come! | | | Dance of the distant stars |
| Come! | | | Soul of all that lives |
| Come! | | | Gift of all that gives |
| Come! | | | Sign of healing and wholeness |
| Come! | | | Silence within our prayer |
| Come! | | | Everlasting Hope |
| Come! | | | Tongues of fire and flame |
| Come! | | | Love that never ends |
| Come! | | | Life of the Living God |
| Come! | | | Wisdom and Understanding |
| Come! | | | Knowledge and Fortitude |
| Come! | | | Caregiver, Comforter |
| Come! | | | Laughter in the midst of tears |
| Come! | | | Protector of the poor |
| Come! | | | Friend of the utterly alone |
| Come! | | | Known and yet Unknown |
| Come! | | | Holy Spirit, come! |

**ALL**     Come, Holy Spirit, come!

## SILENT REFLECTION

*Reflect on the gift you most desire for the carrying out of your ministry, a ministry of service, a ministry of fidelity to the Gospel of Jesus, whatever your calling in life.*

*Trusting that the power of the Spirit is indeed to be poured out on all people, ask aloud for that gift of the Spirit you most desire at this time. In response to each one's petition, all respond:*

**ALL**     Come, Spirit,
                 empower us
                 to be ministers of the Gospel.

# BENEDICTION

| | |
|---|---|
| **LEADER** | May you live forever, |
| **ALL** | May you live forever, |
| **LEADER** | in the name of Love. |
| **ALL** | in the name of Love. |
| **LEADER** | May you love forever, |
| **ALL** | May you love forever, |
| **LEADER** | in the name of Life. |
| **ALL** | in the name of Life. |
| **LEADER** | Called by God, |
| **ALL** | Called by God, |
| **LEADER** | filled with the Spirit, |
| **ALL** | filled with the Spirit, |
| **LEADER** | committed and faithful, |
| **ALL** | committed and faithful, |
| **LEADER** | rejoicing always, |
| **ALL** | rejoicing always, |
| **LEADER** | may you live in love forever. Amen. |
| **ALL** | may you live in love forever. Amen. |

**SONG**  "Come, Spirit" (See page 233.)

# TRANSFORMATION RITUALS

*Embracing Feminine Experience*

**Feminine experience moves through death to life.**

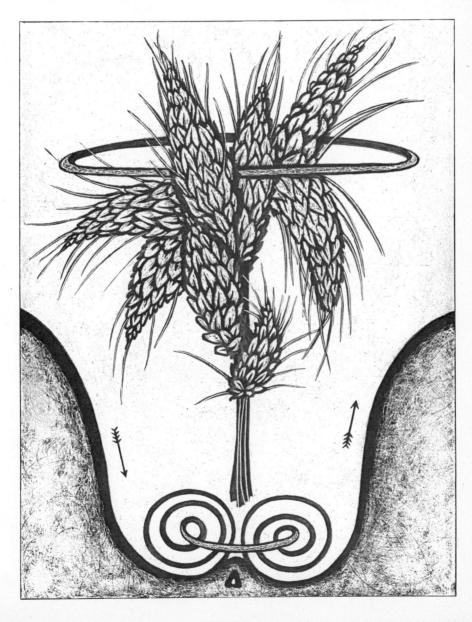

# VALIANT WOMEN

| | |
|---|---|
| **LEADER** | Who shall find a valiant woman? |
| **ALL** | Look! We are all around you: |
| **VOICE** | in the work rooms<br>of industry<br>and of every functioning enterprise,<br>unheralded,<br>invisible,<br>some say nonexistent,<br>but we know otherwise. |
| **LEADER** | Who shall find a valiant woman? |
| **ALL** | Look! We are all around you: |
| **VOICE** | contributing,<br>setting standards,<br>changing the course of history,<br>preparing,<br>supporting,<br>challenging those<br>resentful of our collegial claims<br>and capability. |
| **LEADER** | Who shall find a valiant woman? |
| **ALL** | Look! We are all around you: |
| **VOICE** | women of courage,<br>compassionate,<br>long-suffering, |

|        |                               |
|--------|-------------------------------|
|        | our number is legion,         |
|        | our gifts diverse,            |
|        | our goal one and the same:    |
|        | that history hear,            |
|        | is cognizant of,              |
|        | will one day recall           |
|        | our name.                     |

**LEADER**    Let us move around the group
from person to person
so that everyone here
can hear our name.

*In turn, speak your name aloud in the midst of the assembly (you may prefer first names only).*

**LEADER**    Let us pray:

## SILENT PRAYER

**LEADER**    Living God,
loving God,
we thank You
and we praise You
for the power of Your presence
deep in our hearts,
the vitality of Your presence
here in our midst,
for this opportunity
to come together
to affirm our identity
and to celebrate
our common hope.
We thank You
for the quality of achievement
that is represented here,
for the many and diverse efforts
that continue to contribute
toward the building of a better world.
Pour out Your Spirit upon us.
Confirm and strengthen our vision.
Be the Hope that sustains us
and strengthens us
in these changing,
challenging times.
God of our foremothers,
our God forever,
glory and praise!

**ALL**    Amen.

**ALL SING**    "Women" (See page 236.)

## SILENT PRAYER

**LEADER**　　Throughout history
and at present,
there have been and are
many valiant women,
generous, gifted,
who have given of themselves
for the benefit of many
with little or no recompense.
Reflect on your own experience.
Do you feel that the contributions of women
have been duly recognized and affirmed
by the Church or in society?
Do you feel that your own gifts
and contributions
have been recognized and affirmed?
Give an example, recall an incident
from your experience,
to illustrate your response.

## SILENT REFLECTION

## SHARED REFLECTION

**LEADER**　　As we bring our period of sharing to a close,
let us all sing our opening song.

**ALL SING**　　"Women" (See page 236.)

## SILENT PRAYER

**LEADER**　　In the Book of Proverbs
in the Bible,
there is a well-known text about woman,
a woman of quality
who is clever and kind,
a woman who runs a well-ordered house
and a profitable business as well,
a woman who, quite literally,
seems to have done it all.
While we women want to be affirmed
not simply in terms of what we achieve,
but essentially because of who we are,
it is important to recall
from time to time
in this achievement-oriented,
male-dominated world of ours
that women are also achievers,
that we can do and will do well,
that doing well is a tradition for women,
although one of the best-kept secrets
of the entire civilized world.

Let us reflect then on woman as achiever,
as we listen to a piece of wisdom literature
appropriated from the past.
*(Brief pause for silent prayer.)*

**READER**  Who shall find a valiant woman?
Who shall find a woman of strength?
A pearl of great price is she.
Her associates all have confidence in her
and benefit from her expertise.
She initiates good, not evil,
every day of her life.
She does not neglect her household tasks,
she willingly works with her hands.
Broadminded, her global perspective
is a source of nurture for her.
She rises early, before the dawn,
to prepare food for her family
and organize the tasks of the day.
She considers her options,
then makes her move,
investing the experience she already has
or even profits previously earned.
She works diligently, taking pride
in her inner resources and strengths.
When her gifts are encouraged and their value affirmed,
she will work well into the night,
entering wholeheartedly
into even the menial tasks.
She opens her heart to the needy,
she is generous with the poor,
yet she does not neglect her family's needs
nor priorities of her own.
She is known for her dignity and strength,
and she laughs at the days to come.
She often speaks with wisdom,
and she teaches in a kindly way.
Those who are close to her praise her,
her family and associates and friends:
"Many women succeed or do outstanding things,
but you surpass them all!"
Charm is superficial,
and beauty fades,
but the woman who is wise
is the one to be praised.
May the public sector
value her work,
and may all applaud
her integrity.   *(Based on Prov 31:10-31)*

**LEADER**  Imagine yourself as the woman
who is the subject of this reading.

Imagine these words being spoken of you.
Step into the text, assume the role,
and fill it with your own personality,
your own cultural values,
the particulars of your own life.
Where does the text really "fit" for you?
Where does it rub, and why?
How would you retell the story
to make it even more appropriate for today,
to make it more meaningful for you?
Listen to the text again,
then reflect for a time in silence,
before sharing how you feel.

**READER**

*Read the text again.*

## SILENT REFLECTION

## SHARED REFLECTION

**LEADER**    Many remarkable achievements
are absent from the annals of history
because they were done by women,
and the conclusion is drawn
that nothing was done by women
because nothing is recorded there!
We must keep woman's memory alive,
recall and recover her experiences,
because all women are less visible,
their collective worth less valuable,
when one woman's world disappears.

## LITANY IN PRAISE OF VALIANT WOMEN

**LEADER**    Let us now praise valiant women,
recalling to life
representatives
of all those unsung heroines
whose lives are living testimony
that God
is God
in us.

**ALL**    We praise valiant women,
whose lives give hope to us.

**LEADER**    *Eve,*
the first woman,
mother of all the living,
soul of the human race:

**ALL**    Hail, valiant woman!

**LEADER**    *Noah's wife,*
on an ark
forty days
with all those animals:

**ALL**    Hail, valiant woman!

**LEADER**    *Sarah,*
heart of the covenant,
mother of nations,
who conceived laughter
in her old age:

**ALL**    Hail, valiant woman!

**LEADER**    *Rebecca,*
woman of ingenuity,
achieving her own purposes
in a patriarchal world:

**ALL**    Hail, valiant woman!

**LEADER**    *Rachel,*
who waited
seven years, seven days,
waited for love,
waited for life:

**ALL**    Hail, valiant woman!

**LEADER**    *Asenath,*
Joseph's Egyptian wife,
who merged her foreign ancestry
with the bloodline
of the covenant:

**ALL**    Hail, valiant woman!

**LEADER**    *Hatshepsut,*
Queen of Egypt
during the prosperous Eighteenth Dynasty,
who constructed the great temple
in West Thebes,
whose reign was a reign of peace:

**ALL**    Hail, valiant woman!

**LEADER**    *Nefertiti,*
Queen, coruler of Egypt,
who, with her husband,
introduced into Egypt
the revolutionary notion
of worshiping only one God:

**ALL**    Hail, valiant woman!

**LEADER**    *Mother and sister of Moses,*
and *Pharaoh's daughter,*
whose courage enabled Moses

|  |  |
|---|---|
|  | to live<br>to accomplish the exodus: |
| **ALL** | Hail, valiant women! |
| **LEADER** | *Mahlah, Noah, Hoglah, Milcah*, and *Tirzah*,<br>daughters of Zelophehad,<br>descendants of Asenath and Joseph,<br>who convinced Moses<br>to allow women<br>to receive an inheritance: |
| **ALL** | Hail, valiant women! |
| **LEADER** | *Hannah*,<br>witness to the power<br>of prayer<br>and the consequences<br>of faith: |
| **ALL** | Hail, valiant woman! |
| **LEADER** | *Wise woman of Tekoa*,<br>whom men in authority<br>consulted<br>for the wisdom<br>of her word: |
| **ALL** | Hail, valiant woman! |
| **LEADER** | *Woman of womanly wisdom*,<br>wiser than the wisdom<br>of Solomon,<br>whose mother-love<br>saved her child<br>from the stinging slice<br>of the sword: |
| **ALL** | Hail, valiant woman! |
| **LEADER** | *Theoclea*,<br>disciple of Pythagoras<br>in sixth-century Greece,<br>who was chief priestess<br>at Delphi: |
| **ALL** | Hail, valiant woman! |
| **LEADER** | *Phaenarette*,<br>mother of Socrates,<br>a genius in herbal medicine,<br>a respected midwife<br>and mathematician: |
| **ALL** | Hail, valiant woman! |
| **LEADER** | *Sappho*,<br>writer in ancient Greece, |

who is said to be
one of the greatest poets
who ever lived:

**ALL**      Hail, valiant woman!

**LEADER**      *Huldah,*
prophet in Israel,
whose judgment
shaped the canon
that contains God's holy word:

**ALL**      Hail, valiant woman!

**LEADER**      *All those women of Israel and the ancient Near East,*
who were faithful to their calling,
whose deeds no one remembers,
whose names are unrecorded,
whose lives remain unknown:

**ALL**      Hail, valiant women!

**LEADER**      *Mary,*
mother of Jesus
the Christ,
a woman,
one of us:

**ALL**      Hail, valiant woman!

**LEADER**      *Elizabeth,*
who proved
one is never too old
to have her dream come true:

**ALL**      Hail, valiant woman!

**LEADER**      *Anna,*
prophet at prayer
in the Temple
when Jesus was offered to God,
who from that moment
preached Jesus,
proclaiming salvation to all:

**ALL**      Hail, valiant woman!

**LEADER**      *Mary,*
mother of Joseph and James,
who joined Jesus
in ministry:

**ALL**      Hail, valiant woman!

**LEADER**      *Salome,*
who followed Jesus
and shared in his ministry:

**ALL**      Hail, valiant woman!

| | |
|---|---|
| **LEADER** | *Peter's mother-in-law,*<br>who was cured<br>of a high fever<br>by Jesus<br>and immediately<br>saw to the needs<br>of her guests: |
| **ALL** | Hail, valiant woman! |
| **LEADER** | *Mother of the sons of Zebedee,*<br>who was unafraid to speak her mind,<br>who atoned for her push<br>for power and prestige<br>by standing at the cross: |
| **ALL** | Hail, valiant woman! |
| **LEADER** | *Mary and Martha of Bethany,*<br>soul-friends of Jesus<br>with whom he felt at home<br>and shared his ministry: |
| **ALL** | Hail, valiant women! |
| **LEADER** | *Generous widow,*<br>whom Jesus praised<br>because she gave all she had: |
| **ALL** | Hail, valiant woman! |
| **LEADER** | *Prophetic woman,*<br>who discerned the truth,<br>and proclaimed Jesus<br>Messiah<br>by anointing his head with oil: |
| **ALL** | Hail, valiant woman! |
| **LEADER** | *Woman rebuked by Jesus,*<br>who dared<br>to speak her mind<br>in public<br>at the risk of being put down: |
| **ALL** | Hail, valiant woman! |
| **LEADER** | *Woman servant,*<br>who spoke the truth<br>when Peter lied,<br>swearing<br>that he did not know the man: |
| **ALL** | Hail, valiant woman! |
| **LEADER** | *Pilate's wife,*<br>who begged her husband<br>to trust her intuition<br>and not condemn Jesus to death: |

| | |
|---|---|
| **ALL** | Hail, valiant woman! |
| **LEADER** | *Mary, mother of John Mark,*<br>at whose home<br>in Jerusalem,<br>Christians met to pray: |
| **ALL** | Hail, valiant woman! |
| **LEADER** | *Lydia,*<br>of Macedonia,<br>a business woman<br>converted by Paul,<br>who met with a group for prayer: |
| **ALL** | Hail, valiant woman! |
| **LEADER** | *Phoebe,*<br>deacon of the church in Cenchreae: |
| **ALL** | Hail, valiant woman! |
| **LEADER** | *Mary,*<br>in ministry in the church in Rome: |
| **ALL** | Hail, valiant woman! |
| **LEADER** | *Junia,*<br>in ministry in the church in Rome: |
| **ALL** | Hail, valiant woman! |
| **LEADER** | *Tryphaena and Tryphosa,*<br>in ministry in the church in Rome: |
| **ALL** | Hail, valiant women! |
| **LEADER** | *Persis,*<br>in ministry in the church in Rome: |
| **ALL** | Hail, valiant woman! |
| **LEADER** | *Julia,*<br>in ministry in the church in Rome: |
| **ALL** | Hail, valiant woman! |
| **LEADER** | *Olympas,*<br>in ministry in the church in Rome: |
| **ALL** | Hail, valiant woman! |
| **LEADER** | *Mother of Rufus,*<br>in ministry in the church in Rome: |
| **ALL** | Hail, valiant woman! |
| **LEADER** | *Sister of Nereus,*<br>in ministry in the church in Rome: |
| **ALL** | Hail, valiant woman! |

| | |
|---|---|
| **LEADER** | *Priscilla*,<br>known also as<br>*Prisca*,<br>church leader and teacher,<br>in a team ministry<br>with her husband: |
| **ALL** | Hail, valiant woman! |
| **LEADER** | *Tabitha*,<br>known also as<br>*Dorcas*,<br>a disciple<br>and devoted worker<br>at Joppa,<br>whom Peter raised<br>from the dead: |
| **ALL** | Hail, valiant woman! |
| **LEADER** | *Chloe*,<br>prominent in the Corinthian church: |
| **ALL** | Hail, valiant woman! |
| **LEADER** | *Four women prophets*,<br>daughters of Philip,<br>who preached prophetically: |
| **ALL** | Hail, valiant women! |
| **LEADER** | *Women of Corinth*,<br>who prayed and prophesied<br>in church,<br>whom Paul enjoined<br>to keep silent: |
| **ALL** | Hail, valiant women! |
| **LEADER** | *Rhoda*,<br>maid at the house of Mary,<br>mother of John Mark,<br>who, in her joy<br>at seeing Peter,<br>left him standing<br>at the gate: |
| **ALL** | Hail, valiant woman! |
| **LEADER** | *Claudia*,<br>in ministry in the church: |
| **ALL** | Hail, valiant woman! |
| **LEADER** | *Evodia and Syntyche*,<br>who labored side by side<br>with Paul<br>and Clement<br>and their fellow workers: |

| | |
|---|---|
| **ALL** | Hail, valiant women! |
| **LEADER** | *Nympha,*<br>who had a church at her house<br>in Laodicea: |
| **ALL** | Hail, valiant woman! |
| **LEADER** | *Apphia,*<br>who had a church at her house: |
| **ALL** | Hail, valiant woman! |
| **LEADER** | *Thecla,*<br>declared a legend,<br>perhaps because her reality<br>as role model for women<br>was too much of a threat to all: |
| **ALL** | Hail, valiant woman! |
| **LEADER** | *All those women of the early church*<br>who were truly pioneers,<br>as prophets, preachers,<br>pastoral leaders,<br>following in the footsteps of Jesus: |
| **ALL** | Hail, valiant women! |
| **LEADER** | *Cecilia,*<br>second or third century,<br>one of the most venerated martyrs<br>in the early Roman Church,<br>who today is known as<br>patron of church music: |
| **ALL** | Hail, valiant woman! |
| **LEADER** | *Lucy,*<br>who, according to tradition,<br>witnessed to her faith<br>by giving generously to the poor<br>during an era of Christian persecutions,<br>was denounced by the man<br>to whom she was betrothed,<br>and martyred in the year 303: |
| **ALL** | Hail, valiant woman! |
| **LEADER** | *Monica,*<br>mother of Augustine,<br>who besieged God<br>for his conversion<br>until her prayer was answered,<br>who was influential<br>in the life of her son<br>and the Church<br>because of her piety: |
| **ALL** | Hail, valiant woman! |

**LEADER**    *Proba,*
fourth-century theologian,
whose interpretation of tradition
was systematically ignored:

**ALL**    Hail, valiant woman!

**LEADER**    *Paula,*
scholarly friend of Jerome,
the respected Doctor of the Church,
whose circle of learning for women
in Rome
remains virtually unknown:

**ALL**    Hail, valiant woman!

**LEADER**    *Himiko,*
Queen of Wa,
the first recorded ruler of Japan,
who waged peace in the fourth century
by sending emissaries to China
and by uniting warring tribes and clans:

**ALL**    Hail, valiant woman!

**LEADER**    *Bridget,*
patron saint of Ireland,
who founded a monastic center of learning
for women
in the fifth century
and was influential in politics
and church affairs:

**ALL**    Hail, valiant woman!

**LEADER**    *Khadija,*
Mohammed's first wife,
a successful businesswoman
who had a strong influence
on the prophet,
who supported and encouraged him
during the time of his first revelations:

**ALL**    Hail, valiant woman!

**LEADER**    *Fatimah,*
Mohammed's daughter,
his only surviving child,
held in high esteem
by Muslims,
who was with her father
through his years of persecution:

**ALL**    Hail, valiant woman!

**LEADER**    *Wu Zi-Tien,*
the only woman emperor
of China,

who reigned brilliantly and effectively
for forty years
late in the seventh century,
making Buddhism the state religion
and the Tang Dynasty a liberal interlude
for women:

**ALL**        Hail, valiant woman!

**LEADER**    *Irene*,
self-proclaimed emperor
of Constantinople
at the end of the eighth century,
the first woman
to head the Roman Empire in the East,
who restored religious tolerance
and convoked ecumenical councils
in Constantinople and Nicea:

**ALL**        Hail, valiant woman!

**LEADER**    *Trotula*,
eleventh-century physician,
considered the mother of gynecology,
whose book on women's diseases
was a valuable reference
for centuries after her death:

**ALL**        Hail, valiant woman!

**LEADER**    *Heloise*,
who was banished to a convent
by her husband Abelard
soon after they were married,
who became abbess
and founder of a theological college,
who was one of the great female writers
and perhaps the most learned woman
in twelfth-century France:

**ALL**        Hail, valiant woman!

**LEADER**    *Hildegarde of Bingen*,
twelfth-century mystic,
one of the great minds
of medieval Europe—
abbess, scientist, scholar,
composer, visionary, poet:

**ALL**        Hail, valiant woman!

**LEADER**    *Elizabeth of Hungary*,
thirteenth-century princess
who married a German prince,
reigned as Queen of Thuringia,

bore four children,
was widowed and disowned,
who loved the poor
and ministered to them,
who built a hospital for lepers,
and died at age twenty-four:

**ALL**        Hail, valiant woman!

**LEADER**     *Clare of Assisi,*
a visionary
born of a noble family
in thirteenth-century Italy,
who renounced prosperity,
founded the Poor Clares,
and was Francis of Assisi's
co-worker and friend:

**ALL**        Hail, valiant woman!

**LEADER**     *Julian of Norwich,*
fourteenth century,
England,
whose mystical experiences
are revelations of divine love,
who contributed much
to the church's tradition
of mystical theology:

**ALL**        Hail, valiant woman!

**LEADER**     *Maria Bartola,*
sixteenth century,
Mexico's first female historian,
who recorded her experience
of the brutal Spanish conquest
of her Aztec civilization:

**ALL**        Hail, valiant woman!

**LEADER**     *Katherine Zell,*
sixteenth century,
Germany,
zealous promoter of the Reformation
and supporter of equality
between women and men,
who published a collection
of congregational hymns,
who cared for the sick,
the imprisoned,
and hordes of refugees
displaced by religious warfare:

**ALL**        Hail, valiant woman!

**LEADER**   *Argula von Grumbach*,
sixteenth century,
Bavaria,
imprisoned for her outspoken support
of Luther,
who conducted funerals
without authorization
and led worship services
in her home:

**ALL**   Hail, valiant woman!

**LEADER**   *Elizabeth Hooten*,
seventeenth century,
England,
first Quaker woman convert
and one of the movement's
earliest preachers,
who was a missionary
to the West Indies,
who was imprisoned for her faith:

**ALL**   Hail, valiant woman!

**LEADER**   *Anne Hutchinson*,
Massachusetts Bay,
whose Bible study
and group discussions
led to charges of heresy
and excommunication
from her church
in 1637:

**ALL**   Hail, valiant woman!

**LEADER**   *Mary Fisher*,
missionary,
Quaker,
who dared preach publicly
at Cambridge, England,
in front of the college gate
in 1653:

**ALL**   Hail, valiant woman!

**LEADER**   *Dewens Morrey*,
a Quaker in England,
who in 1657
was whipped in the church
until she bled,
because "a woman
must not speak in church":

**ALL**   Hail, valiant woman!

| | |
|---|---|
| **LEADER** | *Okuni,*<br>a priestess<br>in Japan<br>in the seventeenth century,<br>who developed ceremonial dance forms<br>into Kabuki,<br>traditional Japanese drama,<br>in which women, not men,<br>played both male and female roles: |
| **ALL** | Hail, valiant woman! |
| **LEADER** | *Susanna Wesley,*<br>mother of John<br>and eighteen other children,<br>who taught them all<br>in her household school<br>and led prayer<br>in her home: |
| **ALL** | Hail, valiant woman! |
| **LEADER** | *Barbara Heck,*<br>"mother of American Methodism,"<br>who organized America's first Methodist Society<br>in 1766: |
| **ALL** | Hail, valiant woman! |
| **LEADER** | *Abigail Adams,*<br>patriot, feminist,<br>revolutionary,<br>who protested slavery<br>decades before<br>a movement was organized: |
| **ALL** | Hail, valiant woman! |
| **LEADER** | *Ann Lee,*<br>who in 1774<br>emigrated to America<br>and founded the Shakers,<br>a utopian religious community<br>of utmost simplicity: |
| **ALL** | Hail, valiant woman! |
| **LEADER** | *Phillis Wheatley,*<br>who was purchased as a slave<br>at the age of eight,<br>became the first black poet<br>in America,<br>died in poverty<br>at the age of thirty-one<br>in 1784: |
| **ALL** | Hail, valiant woman! |

| | |
|---|---|
| **LEADER** | *Katherine Ferguson*,<br>former slave,<br>who opened the first Sabbath School<br>in 1793: |
| **ALL** | Hail, valiant woman! |
| **LEADER** | *Elizabeth Bayley Seton*,<br>who in 1809<br>founded the Sisters of Charity,<br>the first American women's religious order,<br>and was officially canonized<br>a saint: |
| **ALL** | Hail, valiant woman! |
| **LEADER** | *Mary Lyon*,<br>who founded Mt. Holyoke Female Seminary<br>in 1809<br>as a model for training women<br>as teachers and missionaries: |
| **ALL** | Hail, valiant woman! |
| **LEADER** | *Kaahumanu*,<br>first female ruler<br>and lawmaker of Hawaii,<br>who abolished restrictive practices<br>and taboos against women<br>early in the nineteenth century<br>and established women's right<br>to an education<br>and other basic rights: |
| **ALL** | Hail, valiant woman! |
| **LEADER** | *Lucretia Mott*,<br>preacher, reformer, feminist,<br>who launched the movement<br>for women's rights<br>at Seneca Falls, New York,<br>in 1848: |
| **ALL** | Hail, valiant woman! |
| **LEADER** | *Elizabeth Cady Stanton*,<br>co-organizer<br>at Seneca Falls,<br>who produced<br>The Woman's Bible: |
| **ALL** | Hail, valiant woman! |
| **LEADER** | *Susan B. Anthony*,<br>who led the women's liberation<br>revolution<br>and pushed for women's right<br>to vote: |

| | |
|---|---|
| **ALL** | Hail, valiant woman! |
| **LEADER** | *Harriet Beecher Stowe,*<br>nineteenth-century<br>New England novelist,<br>whose powerful depiction<br>of the plight of slaves<br>captured the American conscience: |
| **ALL** | Hail, valiant woman! |
| **LEADER** | *Emily Dickinson,*<br>American poet,<br>who was able to transform<br>personal pain<br>into strong, sensitive verse<br>that continues to inspire: |
| **ALL** | Hail, valiant woman! |
| **LEADER** | *Antoinette Brown,*<br>first American woman<br>ordained to ministry,<br>ordained in the Congregational Church<br>in 1853: |
| **ALL** | Hail, valiant woman! |
| **LEADER** | *Elizabeth Blackwell,*<br>first woman in America<br>to graduate from medical school<br>and become a licensed physician,<br>who founded a medical school for women<br>in 1865: |
| **ALL** | Hail, valiant woman! |
| **LEADER** | *Margaret Newton Van Cott,*<br>first woman granted<br>a local preacher's license<br>in the Methodist Episcopal Church,<br>1869: |
| **ALL** | Hail, valiant woman! |
| **LEADER** | *Rosana Chouteau,*<br>North American Indian,<br>elected chief of the Osage Beaver Band<br>in 1875,<br>the first female chief<br>in that patriarchal tribe: |
| **ALL** | Hail, valiant woman! |
| **LEADER** | *Catherine Booth,*<br>outstanding revival preacher,<br>co-founder of the Salvation Army<br>in 1878: |
| **ALL** | Hail, valiant woman! |

**LEADER**      *Anna Howard Shaw,*
first woman ordained
in the Methodist Protestant Church,
1880:

**ALL**      Hail, valiant woman!

**LEADER**      *Clara Barton,*
who served as a nurse
in the Civil War
and founded the American Red Cross
for emergency relief
in 1881:

**ALL**      Hail, valiant woman!

**LEADER**      *Emma Lazarus,*
Jewish poet,
whose words are inscribed
on the Statue of Liberty,
whose poem was chosen
from among submissions by
Longfellow, Whitman, and Twain:

**ALL**      Hail, valiant woman!

**LEADER**      *Sister Blandina Segale,*
pioneer of the American southwest,
who ended the lynch law
and tamed Billy the Kid
at the end of the Santa Fe Trail:

**ALL**      Hail, valiant woman!

**LEADER**      *Pandita Ramabai,*
a Sanskrit scholar
who challenged interpretations
of Hindu law
in order to raise the status of women,
who was a delegate
to the Indian National Congress
in 1889:

**ALL**      Hail, valiant woman!

**LEADER**      *Wilhelmina Elisabeth Drucker,*
of the Netherlands,
who founded the Association of Free Women
in 1889,
and was consequently labeled
"Mad Mina"
because of her zeal for women's rights:

**ALL**      Hail, valiant woman!

**LEADER**      *Ellen Gould White,*
who founded the Seventh-Day Adventists
at the close of the nineteenth century,
after the Adventist movement died:

| | |
|---|---|
| **ALL** | Hail, valiant woman! |
| **LEADER** | *Ida B. Wells-Barnett,*<br>ardent advocate<br>of rights for Blacks,<br>who organized the first<br>black women's suffrage group: |
| **ALL** | Hail, valiant woman! |
| **LEADER** | *Jiu Jin,*<br>revolutionary feminist,<br>poet, teacher<br>in China,<br>executed in 1908<br>for refusing to compromise<br>her beliefs: |
| **ALL** | Hail, valiant woman! |
| **LEADER** | *María Jesús Alvarada Rivera,*<br>who initiated the feminist movement<br>in Peru<br>at the turn of the century;<br>a tireless activist for women's rights,<br>she was imprisoned<br>and eventually exiled: |
| **ALL** | Hail, valiant woman! |
| **LEADER** | *Raden Ajeng Kartini,*<br>who initiated the feminist movement<br>in Indonesia<br>at the turn of the century;<br>outspoken against social and colonial oppression,<br>she started a successful school for girls,<br>and died in childbirth at age twenty-five: |
| **ALL** | Hail, valiant woman! |
| **LEADER** | *Marie Curie,*<br>Nobel prize in physics,<br>Nobel prize in chemistry,<br>first woman to receive<br>a full professorship,<br>in 1906, in France,<br>at the Sorbonne: |
| **ALL** | Hail, valiant woman! |
| **LEADER** | *Mary Baker Eddy,*<br>founder and leader<br>of Christian Science<br>until her death in 1910: |
| **ALL** | Hail, valiant woman! |

| | |
|---|---|
| **LEADER** | *Käthe Kollwitz,*<br>graphic artist and sculptor,<br>twentieth century,<br>Berlin,<br>whose empathy<br>for the working class<br>permeates her works on<br>poverty, death, hunger,<br>and war: |
| **ALL** | Hail, valiant woman! |
| **LEADER** | *Jovita Idar,*<br>organized the first Mexican Congress,<br>Texas, 1911,<br>was president of the Mexican Feminist League: |
| **ALL** | Hail, valiant woman! |
| **LEADER** | *Me Katilili,*<br>who at age seventy,<br>organized the Giriama tribe's<br>movement for independence<br>from British rule,<br>in Kenya,<br>in 1911: |
| **ALL** | Hail, valiant woman! |
| **LEADER** | *Phoebe Palmer,*<br>major force behind the Holiness Movement,<br>spiritual mother of Pilgrim Holiness Church<br>and Church of the Nazarene: |
| **ALL** | Hail, valiant woman! |
| **LEADER** | *Aimee Semple McPherson,*<br>a twentieth-century preacher<br>famous for her<br>"Foursquare Gospel Church"<br>in the Pentecostal movement: |
| **ALL** | Hail, valiant woman! |
| **LEADER** | *Madame C. J. Walker,*<br>who worked eighteen years<br>as a washerwoman<br>before becoming<br>the first female black American<br>millionaire: |
| **ALL** | Hail, valiant woman! |
| **LEADER** | *Kasturba,*<br>wife of Mahatma Gandhi,<br>from whom he learned<br>the basic concept<br>of nonviolent resistance: |
| **ALL** | Hail, valiant woman! |

**LEADER**   *Helen Keller,*
born without sight or hearing,
graduated from Radcliffe with honors,
mastered several languages,
published a series of books:

**ALL**   Hail, valiant woman!

**LEADER**   *Mary McLeod Bethune,*
black educator, leader, reformer,
who founded a college
that has influenced many
and established the National Council
of Negro Women
in 1935:

**ALL**   Hail, valiant woman!

**LEADER**   *Dorothy Day,*
cofounder of the Catholic Worker Movement,
a prophetic witness
to the social gospel
and a true friend
of the poor:

**ALL**   Hail, valiant woman!

**LEADER**   *Noor un Nissa,*
a young Muslim woman,
who was known as the heroic "Madeleine"
of the French Resistance
during World War II
and is the only woman to receive
both the George Cross
and the Croix de Guerre:

**ALL**   Hail, valiant woman!

**LEADER**   *Regina Jonas,*
first woman rabbi,
although never officially ordained;
when ordination was denied
because of her sex,
she was granted a diploma
privately,
and not long after,
in 1940,
died in a concentration camp:

**ALL**   Hail, valiant woman!

**LEADER**   *Li Tim Oi,*
first woman ordained
in the Anglican tradition,
Hong Kong,
1944,
but her ordination

|           |                                                                                                         |
|-----------|---------------------------------------------------------------------------------------------------------|
|           | was officially rejected,<br>and she subsequently resigned:                                              |
| **ALL**   | Hail, valiant woman!                                                                                     |
| **LEADER**| *Maud Keister Jensen*,<br>first woman to receive<br>full clergy rights<br>in the Methodist Church,<br>1956: |
| **ALL**   | Hail, valiant woman!                                                                                     |
| **LEADER**| *Wilma Rudolph*,<br>who became known as<br>"the world's fastest woman"<br>after the 1960 Olympics<br>in Rome,<br>where she became the first American woman<br>to win three gold medals: |
| **ALL**   | Hail, valiant woman!                                                                                     |
| **LEADER**| *Valentina Tereshkova*,<br>of Russia,<br>who became the first woman cosmonaut<br>in space<br>in 1963:   |
| **ALL**   | Hail, valiant woman!                                                                                     |
| **LEADER**| *Shirley Chisholm*,<br>who in 1968<br>became the first black woman<br>to be elected<br>to the U.S. House of Representatives: |
| **ALL**   | Hail, valiant woman!                                                                                     |
| **LEADER**| *Elizabeth Platz*,<br>first woman ordained<br>in the Lutheran Church in America,<br>1970:               |
| **ALL**   | Hail, valiant woman!                                                                                     |
| **LEADER**| *Erin Pizzey*,<br>a housewife<br>who formed Women's Aid,<br>the first shelter<br>for battered women<br>in Great Britain: |
| **ALL**   | Hail, valiant woman!                                                                                     |
| **LEADER**| *Sally Priesand*,<br>first woman rabbi ordained<br>from any Jewish theological seminary,<br>1972:       |

| | |
|---|---|
| **ALL** | Hail, valiant woman! |
| **LEADER** | *Nancy Wittig, Betty Schiess,* *Merrill Bittner, Alla Bozarth-Campbell,* *Jeanette Piccard, Alison Cheek,* *Marie Moorfield, Katrina Swanson,* *Carter Heyward, Suzanne Hiatt,* *and Emily Hewitt,* *first American women ordained* *to the Episcopal priesthood,* *Philadelphia, 1974,* *first Episcopal ordination of women* *to be officially recognized:* |
| **ALL** | Hail, valiant women! |
| **LEADER** | *Junko Tabei,* of Japan, the first woman to scale Mount Everest, 1975: |
| **ALL** | Hail, valiant woman! |
| **LEADER** | *Betty Williams and Mairead Corrigan,* who organized the people's movement for peace in Northern Ireland in 1976 and were awarded the Nobel prize: |
| **ALL** | Hail, valiant women! |
| **LEADER** | *The madres and abuelas,* mothers and grandmothers of Argentina, who have kept vigil in the Plaza de Mayo since March 1977 in order to protest the torture and disappearance of their children and other loved ones: |
| **ALL** | Hail, valiant women! |
| **LEADER** | *Helen Joseph,* South Africa, anti-apartheid activist and outspoken feminist, arrested for civil disobedience in 1956, arrested for supporting Winnie Mandela in 1977: |
| **ALL** | Hail, valiant woman! |

| LEADER | *Marjorie Matthews,* first woman bishop of the United Methodist Church, the first woman bishop of any major denomination in modern times, who served in Wisconsin from 1980 and died in 1986: |
|---|---|
| **ALL** | Hail, valiant woman! |
| **LEADER** | *Naheed,* a schoolgirl in Afghanistan, who led a demonstration against the Soviet invasion of her country, April 1980, and was one of seventy children to be massacred: |
| **ALL** | Hail, valiant woman! |
| **LEADER** | *Leontyne Kelly,* second woman bishop, the first black woman bishop in the United Methodist Church, San Francisco, 1984: |
| **ALL** | Hail, valiant woman! |
| **LEADER** | *Indira Gandhi,* prime minister of India, who was elected twice to that position and assassinated while in office: |
| **ALL** | Hail, valiant woman! |
| **LEADER** | *Samantha Smith,* American schoolgirl, goodwill ambassador to Russia at the age of eleven, who died in a plane crash at age thirteen in 1985: |
| **ALL** | Hail, valiant woman! |
| **LEADER** | *All women in ministry,* ordained and unordained, all who were first to pave the way and all who followed after: |
| **ALL** | Hail, valiant women! |

| LEADER | *All women of accomplishment,*<br>who achieved<br>despite the odds,<br>in science, the arts,<br>religion, health,<br>education, economics,<br>athletics, and the<br>sociopolitical fields: |
|---|---|
| **ALL** | Hail, valiant women! |
| **LEADER** | Who shall find a valiant woman? |
| **ALL** | Look! We are all around you. |

*The Leader invites participants to name women they wish to single out for recognition. Call out names spontaneously. When the naming has ceased all respond:*

| **LEADER** | Hail, valiant women! |
|---|---|
| **ALL** | Hail, valiant women! |
| **LEADER** | Inspired by this witness<br>of our sisters in faith,<br>let us now go forth encouraged<br>to give of our best efforts,<br>knowing that the grace of God<br>is power unto good. |

## BENEDICTION

| **LEADER** | May goodness flow<br>from the work of your (our) hands,<br>by the God of your (our) mother<br>who will help you (us),<br>by God Shaddai who will bless you (us)<br>with blessings of heaven,<br>blessings of the deep,<br>blessings of the breasts<br>and of the womb;<br>for the blessings of God<br>are mighty<br>beyond the blessings<br>of the eternal mountains<br>and the bounties<br>of the everlasting hills.<br>Blessed be God!   *(Gen 49:25-26)* |
|---|---|
| **ALL** | Amen! |
| **SONG** | "A New Day Dawns" (See page 239.) |

# OUT OF EXILE

| | |
|---|---|
| **LEADER** | All who are in bondage, cry: |
| **ALL** | Lead us out of exile!<br>Deliver us from evil! |
| **LEADER** | All who are exploited, cry: |
| **ALL** | Lead us out of exile!<br>Deliver us from evil! |
| **LEADER** | All who loath oppression, cry: |
| **ALL** | Lead us out of exile!<br>Deliver us from evil! |
| **LEADER** | Behold, now is the acceptable time,<br>the time of our liberation.<br>We are a chosen people,<br>we are a holy nation.<br>All of us who are in Christ,<br>we are a new creation.<br>*(2 Cor 6:2; 1 Pet 2:9; 2 Cor 5:17)* |
| **LEADER** | Let us pray: |

## SILENT PRAYER

| | |
|---|---|
| **LEADER** | God of the Exodus,<br>hear the cry<br>of all Your suffering people,<br>women who hunger,<br>women who hurt, |

women who are despised.
Long have we been in exile,
cut off from our roots
in the holy places
because we are feminine.
Lift the burden
of gender
and class
and lead us into freedom,
where all are one
in spirit and truth.
Let everyone say:

**ALL**       Amen!

**READER**   The following text
from the canon of scripture
is taken from the Book of Judges.
Listen to the biblical narrative,
and discern the word of God!

In those days,
when there was no king in Israel,
a Levite who lived in Ephraim
took as his concubine
a woman from Bethlehem.
One day, in anger,
she left him
and returned to her father's house.
After four months had passed,
her husband set out
to fetch her
and bring her back.
His father-in-law greeted him
joyfully
and invited him to stay awhile.
He ate and drank
and spent the night
and after three days
prepared to leave,
but his father-in-law insisted
he stay a little longer.
The fourth day passed,
and the fifth day;
then finally,
toward evening,
determined to delay no longer,
he set out with his donkeys
and his concubine
and his servant.
As they drew near to Jerusalem,
his servant said,

"Master, let us spend the night."
"Not here, in a town of foreigners,"
he replied.
"Let us continue on to Gibeah
and tarry among Israelites."
They reached Gibeah
as the sun was setting,
but no one offered hospitality,
so they sat down in the public square.
An old man,
returning from the fields,
not a native of Gibeah
but a sojourner from Ephraim
who had settled in the town,
saw the travelers
and stopped to inquire:
"Where have you come from?
Where are you going?"
"We are on our way
from Bethlehem in Judah
to Ephraim, my home,
but no one has offered us shelter
for the night.
We have enough provisions,
straw for the donkeys,
and bread and wine."
The old man answered,
"Shalom! Come with me.
I will see to all your needs.
You cannot spend the night
out here in the public square."
So he took them home,
where they washed their feet
and were made comfortable.
As they were at table,
men from the town,
abusive and drunk,
surrounded the house
and beat on the door,
demanding that the guest
be sent out to them
that they might have sex with him.
The old man pleaded,
"My brothers, no,
this man is my guest,
do not commit this crime.
Here is my daughter,
a virgin, a child;
I will give her over to you.
Enjoy her,
do what you please with her,

but do not violate the man."
The men would not listen,
they were out of control;
so the Levite, the guest,
took his concubine
and brought her out to them.
They raped her,
savagely,
again and again,
abusing her
until morning.
At daybreak,
they let her go,
and she fell at the threshold
of the old man's house
and lay there
without moving.
When the sun was up,
her husband arose,
and opened the door,
prepared to continue his journey.
Seeing her, he said,
"Get up! We must go."
She was silent.
She was dead.
He laid her across his donkey
and journeyed to his home.
When he reached his house,
he took a knife
and dissected his concubine,
limb by limb,
cut her up into twelve pieces,
and sent her mutilated body
throughout all of Israel.
He instructed his messengers
to say to the people:
"Has any man
seen such a thing
from the time of the Exodus
until now?
Reflect on this,
discuss it,
then tell me what you decide."
All who saw it said,
"Never!
Never has such a thing been done,
never has such a thing been seen
since the time of the Exodus."   *(Judg 19:1-30)*

**LEADER**       We have just heard a biblical story,
and we have been taught

that the Bible is the word of God.
How do you feel about what you heard?
What could be the point of such a story
in which women are devalued
and physically abused?
Is there any meaning here for us
and for the times in which we live?
Reflect for a while
before you respond.

## SILENT REFLECTION

## SHARED REFLECTION

*When the sharing has subsided, the leader invites the group to share personal experiences.*

**LEADER**    Give an example
from your own experience
or your awareness of another's experience
to illustrate
the abuse, exploitation, oppression
of women
all over the world
today.

## SHARED EXPERIENCE

## LITANY IN REMEMBRANCE OF VIOLATED WOMEN

**LEADER**    Let us remember violated women,
calling to mind
representatives
of all our suffering sisters
whose experience
is rooted
in death to life
and whose witness lives
in us.

**ALL**    We remember violated women,
whose pain lives on in us.

**LEADER**    All the so-called
*"daughters of men"*
who married the legendary
"sons of God,"
whose lives have been obliterated,
whose daughters are unnamed and unknown,
whose male progeny recorded history
and claimed it as their own:

**ALL**    Sisters, we remember you.

| | |
|---|---|
| **LEADER** | *Hagar,*<br>Sarah's maid,<br>who bore the child of Abraham<br>and suffered banishment: |
| **ALL** | Sister, we remember you. |
| **LEADER** | *Lot's wife and daughters,*<br>victims of violence<br>and degradation<br>in a world that favored men: |
| **ALL** | Sisters, we remember you. |
| **LEADER** | *Dinah,*<br>sister of a dozen brothers,<br>scarred by their code of violence<br>in a very violent world: |
| **ALL** | Sister, we remember you. |
| **LEADER** | *Woman of Bethlehem,*<br>defiled<br>and destroyed<br>by a drunken mob<br>and her husband<br>and his host: |
| **ALL** | Sister, we remember you. |
| **LEADER** | *Ahinoam,*<br>wife of Saul<br>the king,<br>married to a man<br>who was either at war<br>or psychotically depressed: |
| **ALL** | Sister, we remember you. |
| **LEADER** | *Tamar,*<br>David's daughter,<br>raped by her brother Amnon<br>and abandoned to her shame: |
| **ALL** | Sister, we remember you. |
| **LEADER** | *Woman who loved much,*<br>whose tears washed the feet of Jesus,<br>whose sincerity touched his heart,<br>whom Luke simply calls<br>"a sinner,"<br>whom the Pharisees<br>despised: |
| **ALL** | Sister, we remember you. |

| | |
|---|---|
| **LEADER** | *Woman accused of adultery*, whom Jesus saved from a mob of men preparing to throw their stones: |
| **ALL** | Sister, we remember you. |
| **LEADER** | *Syrophoenician woman*, foreigner in Israel, subjected to insults, rejected, ignored when she sought her daughter's cure: |
| **ALL** | Sister, we remember you. |
| **LEADER** | *Weeping women of Jerusalem*, who faithfully followed the way of the Cross: |
| **ALL** | Sisters, we remember you. |
| **LEADER** | *Slave girl in Philippi*, liberated by Paul, who had been kept in bondage by those who exploited her: |
| **ALL** | Sister, we remember you. |
| **LEADER** | *All women in the apostolic Church*, whose deeds have been obliterated, whose leadership has been denied, who were victims of patriarchal arrogance, whose vision seems to have died: |
| **ALL** | Sisters, we remember you. |
| **LEADER** | *All women saints and martyrs*, who died in the Roman arena, who were raped and tortured and slain, whose spirit died through discrimination, and longs to rise again: |
| **ALL** | Sisters, we remember you. |
| **LEADER** | *All women who have protested*, who challenged unjust structures, who were persecuted for their stance, who were cut off from their source of nurture and given no second chance: |
| **ALL** | Sisters, we remember you. |
| **ALL SING** | "One By One" (See page 241.) |
| **LEADER** | My sisters, let us pray: |
| **ALL** | Our Mother, on earth and in heaven: holy is Your name. |

May Your wisdom come,
Your will be done,
here and now,
as it was in the beginning.
Give us today our nurturing bread,
and forgive us our rage,
as we forgive those
who discriminate against us.
Let us not become self-righteous,
but deliver us from bondage.
For Yours is the wisdom
and compassion
and Mother-love forever.
Amen.

## SILENT PRAYER

**READING**   As we listen to the prophet Isaiah,
we hear the Messiah speaking to us,
promising to lead us out of exile,
lifting us up with hope.

O afflicted one,
storm-tossed,
disconsolate,
behold I will lay your foundations
with jewels,
your gates
with precious metals,
your walls
with precious stones.
All your daughters
will be taught by God
and will know prosperity.
You will be rooted
in justice,
far from all oppression,
immune to attack
or terror.
You will have nothing to fear.   *(Is 54:11-14)*
   *(Pause)*

Hear me,
you who cry out for deliverance,
you who turn to God:
you will go forth in joy,
you will be led in peace,
and the mountains and hills
will break into song,
and all the trees
will clap their hands.
For behold,

I create new heavens
and a new earth;
the past will not be remembered,
nor its pain be brought to mind.
You will be glad
and rejoice forever
in what I will create.
No more will be heard
the sound of weeping,
no more will be heard
the cry of distress.
They will not hurt,
they will not destroy,
in all my holy mountain.   *(Is 51:1; 55:12; 65:17-19,25)*
   *(Pause)*

**LEADER**    Let us reflect
with gratitude
on these words of hope.
After a time of quiet prayer,
let us share with one another
from our own experience,
or our awareness of another's experience,
an incident, a memory,
that carries a message of hope,
that symbolizes liberation,
something that says to women today:
God is leading us out of exile.

## SILENT REFLECTION

## SHARED EXPERIENCE

## LITANY OF LIBERATED WOMEN

**LEADER**    Let us praise liberated women,
random representatives
of all women
whose liberation mirrors
the God
who is liberating
us.

**ALL**    We praise liberated women,
who give leadership to us.

**LEADER**    *Leah*,
unlovely
and unloved,
who never let rejection
drive her to defeat:

**ALL**    Hail, liberated woman!

| | |
|---|---|
| **LEADER** | *Tamar*,<br>whose cleverness<br>and determination<br>outwitted Judah,<br>Jacob's son: |
| **ALL** | Hail, liberated woman! |
| **LEADER** | *Shiprah and Purah*,<br>Hebrew midwives<br>in Egypt,<br>who defied Pharaoh's orders<br>and let male babies live: |
| **ALL** | Hail, liberated women! |
| **LEADER** | *Zipporah*,<br>who married Moses<br>and left her home in Midian<br>for exile in Egypt,<br>and saved the life of her husband<br>from God's avenging angel: |
| **ALL** | Hail, liberated woman! |
| **LEADER** | *Miriam*,<br>a prophet,<br>sister of Moses and Aaron,<br>who recorded the Exodus miracle<br>in an epochal victory song,<br>and helped lead the people<br>through their wilderness wandering: |
| **ALL** | Hail, liberated woman! |
| **LEADER** | *Rahab*,<br>by trade a harlot,<br>whose bravery is recorded<br>in the conquest of the promised land: |
| **ALL** | Hail, liberated woman! |
| **LEADER** | *Deborah*,<br>a prophet<br>and a judge in Israel,<br>a leader of armies,<br>a singer of songs: |
| **ALL** | Hail, liberated woman! |
| **LEADER** | *Jael*,<br>who slew an army general<br>and liberated Israel<br>from imminent tyranny: |
| **ALL** | Hail, liberated woman! |

| | |
|---|---|
| **LEADER** | *"A certain woman"* —<br>we have no name—<br>who with a millstone<br>overcame Abimelech,<br>the powerful oppressor<br>who ruled over Israel: |
| **ALL** | Hail, liberated woman! |
| **LEADER** | *Delilah*,<br>who took on Samson,<br>the indestructible,<br>and managed to bring him down: |
| **ALL** | Hail, liberated woman! |
| **LEADER** | *Ruth* and *Naomi*,<br>daughter-in-law,<br>mother-in-law,<br>whose commitment to each other<br>transformed the pain of exile: |
| **ALL** | Hail, liberated women! |
| **LEADER** | *Michal*,<br>Saul's daughter,<br>who helped her husband,<br>David,<br>escape her father's wrath: |
| **ALL** | Hail, liberated woman! |
| **LEADER** | *Abigail*,<br>who convinced David<br>to spare the life<br>of her husband<br>and her household: |
| **ALL** | Hail, liberated woman! |
| **LEADER** | *Witch of Endor*,<br>who recognized Saul<br>through his disguise,<br>and dared to call up Samuel<br>to announce Saul's death: |
| **ALL** | Hail, liberated woman! |
| **LEADER** | *Wise Woman of Abel*,<br>whom men in authority consulted,<br>who liberated the town<br>from Joab's seige: |
| **ALL** | Hail, liberated woman! |
| **LEADER** | *Maid to Naaman's wife*,<br>who dared tell her Syrian master |

|            | that the God of Israel<br>could cure his leprosy: |
|------------|---------------------------------------------------|
| **ALL**    | Hail, liberated woman!                            |
| **LEADER** | *Vashti the Queen*,<br>who refused to parade<br>her beauty before men<br>at the command<br>of her husband,<br>the king: |
| **ALL**    | Hail, liberated woman!                            |
| **LEADER** | *Esther*,<br>symbol of woman's ability<br>to save her world<br>from destruction: |
| **ALL**    | Hail, liberated woman!                            |
| **LEADER** | *Judith*,<br>symbol of woman's ability<br>to make the most<br>of her gift: |
| **ALL**    | Hail, liberated woman!                            |
| **LEADER** | *Mary of Magdala*,<br>follower of Jesus,<br>first witness to the Resurrection,<br>leader in the early Church: |
| **ALL**    | Hail, liberated woman!                            |
| **LEADER** | *Joanna*,<br>wife of Herod's steward,<br>follower of Jesus<br>and member of his company: |
| **ALL**    | Hail, liberated woman!                            |
| **LEADER** | *Susanna*,<br>follower of Jesus,<br>member of his company: |
| **ALL**    | Hail, liberated woman!                            |
| **LEADER** | All those *"many others,"*<br>women who followed Jesus,<br>whom scripture does not name: |
| **ALL**    | Hail, liberated women!                            |
| **LEADER** | *Woman with a hemorrhage*,<br>who touched the garment of Jesus<br>and was touched by his healing power: |
| **ALL**    | Hail, liberated woman!                            |

| LEADER | *Woman bent double*, |
| | overcome with infirmity |
| | and the crippling status of women, |
| | whom Jesus healed on the Sabbath, |
| | which was against the law: |
| ALL | Hail, liberated woman! |
| LEADER | *Woman at the well*, |
| | a Samaritan, |
| | one who was despised, |
| | whom Jesus approached |
| | and commissioned |
| | to preach |
| | the Good News of living water |
| | and of worship in spirit and truth: |
| ALL | Hail, liberated woman! |
| LEADER | *Widow of Nain*, |
| | whose sorrow |
| | at the death |
| | of her only son |
| | became joy when Jesus |
| | raised him to life: |
| ALL | Hail, liberated woman! |
| LEADER | *Daughter of Jairus*, |
| | whom Jesus |
| | raised from the dead: |
| ALL | Hail, liberated woman! |
| LEADER | *Damaris*, |
| | woman of Athens, |
| | converted by Paul |
| | after hearing him preach |
| | in the Areopagus: |
| ALL | Hail, liberated woman! |
| LEADER | *Elect lady* and her |
| | *elect sister*,— |
| | whether really church leaders |
| | or feminine symbols |
| | of a gathered community, |
| | their names bear witness |
| | to the power |
| | of feminine reality: |
| ALL | Hail, liberated women! |
| LEADER | *Marcella*, |
| | founder of a center of learning |
| | for women |
| | in fourth-century Rome, |

well known
for her biblical expertise,
who traveled
and taught
and preached:

**ALL**     Hail, liberated woman!

**LEADER**  *Melania the Younger*,
fourth-century theologian,
who debated doctrine
and taught the emperor,
Theodosius:

**ALL**     Hail, liberated woman!

**LEADER**  *Egeria*,
early fifth-century pilgrim,
whose diary of her travels
to the Holy Land
is a resource to this day:

**ALL**     Hail, liberated woman!

**LEADER**  *Theodora*,
married to the Emperor
Justinian,
Empress of Byzantium,
who raised the low status of women,
helped them inherit property,
set a penalty for rape:

**ALL**     Hail, liberated woman!

**LEADER**  *Lioba*,
eighth-century saint,
associate of Bishop Boniface,
skilled in theology and canon law,
whose authority brought order
to Germany's mission church:

**ALL**     Hail, liberated woman!

**LEADER**  *Catherine of Siena*,
fourteenth-century feminist,
the first of two women named
Doctor of the Church,
deeply involved
in political affairs,
influential in the pope's return
from Avignon to Rome:

**ALL**     Hail, liberated woman!

**LEADER**  *Teresa of Avila*,
sixteenth-century Carmelite nun,

mystic, reformer,
Doctor of the Church:

**ALL**     Hail, liberated woman!

**LEADER**  *Louise de Marillac*,
who founded the Daughters of Charity
in 1633,
opening up a whole new ministry
for women,
whose initiative was suppressed
by Rome
before it was approved,
who found a way
to transcend the rules
and their restrictive consequences:

**ALL**     Hail, liberated woman!

**LEADER**  *Molly Pitcher*,
heroine
of the Revolutionary War:

**ALL**     Hail, liberated woman!

**LEADER**  *Sarah Osborn*,
actively involved
in the Great Awakening,
who invited Blacks
into her home
for Bible study and prayer,
threatening
the establishment:

**ALL**     Hail, liberated woman!

**LEADER**  *Josefa De Dominguez*,
eighteenth-century heroine
of Mexico's independence movement:

**ALL**     Hail, liberated woman!

**LEADER**  *Mary Musgrove*,
eighteenth-century Creek Indian chief,
important political leader
in the history of her tribe,
who facilitated alliances
between her people
and the state of Georgia:

**ALL**     Hail, liberated woman!

**LEADER**  *Lucy Wright*,
central to Shaker ministry,
whose leadership
gave rise to

| | a long, strong female line, |
|---|---|
| | whose songs, dances, and union marches |
| | are hallmarks of Shaker life: |
| **ALL** | Hail, liberated woman! |
| **LEADER** | *Laura Smith Haviland*, |
| | agent of the Underground Railroad, |
| | a fierce, courageous fighter |
| | for the freedom and rehabilitation |
| | of Blacks: |
| **ALL** | Hail, liberated woman! |
| **LEADER** | *Prudence Crandall*, |
| | nineteenth-century pioneer |
| | for the education of black girls |
| | in the North, |
| | who was persecuted |
| | for her stance: |
| **ALL** | Hail, liberated woman! |
| **LEADER** | *Sojourner Truth*, |
| | abolitionist, |
| | reformer, |
| | advocate of women's rights, |
| | a slave who gained her freedom |
| | in 1827 |
| | and traveled the country |
| | preaching |
| | that God was loving and kind: |
| **ALL** | Hail, liberated woman! |
| **LEADER** | *Harriet Tubman*, |
| | born into slavery, |
| | escaped to the North |
| | in 1849, |
| | her Underground Railroad |
| | led more than 300 people |
| | from slavery to freedom, |
| | her people called her "Moses," |
| | for her capture |
| | they offered |
| | a $40,000 reward: |
| **ALL** | Hail, liberated woman! |
| **LEADER** | *Florence Nightingale*, |
| | who raised the menial role |
| | of nurse |
| | to the level of a profession |
| | in nineteenth-century England |
| | and laid the foundation |
| | for nursing as we know it now: |
| **ALL** | Hail, liberated woman! |

| | |
|---|---|
| **LEADER** | *Mary Jones,*<br>Mother Jones,<br>a major organizer<br>in the labor movement,<br>devoted to fostering the dignity<br>of the worker,<br>who died in 1930<br>at 100 years of age: |
| **ALL** | Hail, liberated woman! |
| **LEADER** | *Anna Dengel,*<br>physician,<br>founder of the Medical Mission Sisters<br>in 1925,<br>whose pioneer work<br>among Muslim women<br>caused Rome to change its canon law<br>to allow women and men with religious vows<br>to study medicine,<br>and for the first time,<br>practice it<br>in its full scope: |
| **ALL** | Hail, liberated woman! |
| **LEADER** | *Simone de Beauvoir,*<br>whose feminist manifesto<br>has had a liberating effect<br>on us all: |
| **ALL** | Hail, liberated woman! |
| **LEADER** | *Rosa Parks,*<br>Montgomery, Alabama,<br>whose refusal to give up<br>her seat on a bus<br>in 1955<br>launched the U.S. civil rights movement<br>for all black women and men: |
| **ALL** | Hail, liberated woman! |
| **LEADER** | *Corazon Aquino,*<br>her refusal to yield<br>to dictatorship<br>and her courage in the face of<br>overwhelming odds<br>is a model for all women: |
| **ALL** | Hail, liberated woman! |
| **LEADER** | *Winnie Mandela,*<br>anti-apartheid champion,<br>symbol of hope<br>and bravery<br>and dedication to a cause: |
| **ALL** | Hail, liberated woman! |

| | |
|---|---|
| **ALL SING** | "One By One" (Verses 1 and 5; see page 241.) |
| **LEADER** | We are ministers of a new covenant: |
| **ALL** | We are coming out of exile! |
| **LEADER** | We are afflicted, but not crushed: |
| **ALL** | We are coming out of exile! |
| **LEADER** | We are puzzled, but we do not despair: |
| **ALL** | We are coming out of exile! |
| **LEADER** | We are persecuted, but not overcome: |
| **ALL** | We are coming out of exile! |
| **LEADER** | We are struck down, but not destroyed: |
| **ALL** | We are coming out of exile! |
| **LEADER** | We bear in our bodies the death of Jesus, that his life might show forth in us: |
| **ALL** | We are coming out of exile! *(2 Cor 3:6; 4:8-10)* |
| **LEADER** | Together, let us affirm our faith in the God of our liberation. |

## CREED

**ALL**

I believe in a God
of the womb
and breasts
flowing with the milk of compassion
in times of particular need,
who is not at all involved in writing rules
and regulations,
who is not a stringent taskmaster,
who never wrote a creed.

I believe in a God
who does not enjoy
or condone
exploitation,
who does not set out to conquer
but comes to support
and serve,
who suffers whenever
humanity suffers,
who dies a little whenever Her body
is violated,
mutilated,
or handled with disrespect,
who stands beside and within us
whenever we lose our nerve.

I believe in a God
whose spirit survives
all forms of degradation,
who mediates hope
that rises above the limits
of time
and place,
who is durable
and vulnerable,
who sometimes shows a masculine mood,
more often
a feminine face.

I believe in a God
who holds us all
in Her everlasting arms,
who gathers us protectively
to the shelter of Her wings,
who binds our wounds,
dries our tears,
and promises better things.

## BENEDICTION

**LEADER**    May God direct our going forth
by making a way through the waters.
May She journey with us
in fire and cloud
on our exodus from exile.
May She shorten our wilderness wandering
and bring us to
the promised land
of freedom for all.

**ALL**    Amen.

**SONG**    "One By One" (See page 241.)

# CHOOSE LIFE

| | |
|---|---|
| **LEADER** | Thus says El Shaddai,<br>our God:<br>"I set before you<br>life and death,<br>blessing and curse;<br>therefore, choose life,<br>that you and your children<br>may live." *(Dt 30:19)* |
| **VOICE** | We say to ourselves: |
| **ALL** | Choose life,<br>that you and your children may live. |
| **VOICE** | We say to our friends: |
| **ALL** | Choose life,<br>that you and your children may live. |
| **VOICE** | We say to the world: |
| **ALL** | Choose life,<br>that you and your children may live. |
| **LEADER** | Thus says Jesus,<br>the Word of Shaddai:<br>"I have come<br>that you may have life<br>and have it in abundance." *(Jn 10:10)* |
| **VOICE** | The earth is our source of survival.<br>Deplete her resources, poison her waters,<br>and you will cultivate death. |

| ALL | Choose life, |
| | that you and your children may live. |

| VOICE | The universe is our sacred canopy. |
| | Clutter its space with the hardware of war, |
| | and the stars and the planets will die. |

| ALL | Choose life, |
| | that you and your children may live. |

| VOICE | Life is a fragile environment. |
| | Upset the balance, and everything, everyone, |
| | everywhere will disappear. |

| ALL | Choose life, |
| | that you and your children may live. |

| LEADER | Let us pray: |

## SILENT PRAYER

**LEADER**  God, Creator
and Sustainer of Life,
we the living praise You;
our hearts and our flesh
sing for joy
as we join with all of creation
in a canticle of thanksgiving
for the blessings
of the universe,
the habitat of all that lives.
Forgive our wanton
and wasteful use
of those good and precious resources
entrusted to our care.
Send forth Your Spirit,
renew the earth
as You renew its caretakers,
for we
and all of creation
cry:
Come, Creator Spirit!
Come, Soul of the Universe!
Come, Source of All that Lives!
Come, live in us!

**ALL**  Amen!

## SILENT REFLECTION

**VOICE**  Cherish the earth
and the universe,
from whom we discover how
to live
and, to some extent, why
we die:

we learn that the cycle of death-to-life
that encompasses
night-into-morning,
winter-to-spring,
seed-into-fruit-for-the-harvest
is a fundamental rhythm within
every living thing.

READER    Truly, I say to you,
unless a grain of wheat
falls into the earth
and dies,
it is not viable;
but if it dies,
it bears much fruit.
Whoever really loves her life,
loses it.   *(Jn 12:24-25)*

**ALL SING**

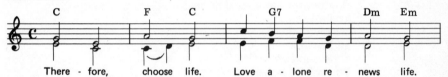

There - fore,    choose life.    Love a - lone re - news life.

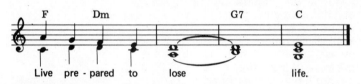

Live pre - pared to lose life.

Miriam Therese Winter
Copyright © Medical Mission Sisters, 1982

READER    To choose life means
to lose life.
Jesus laid down his life for us;
let us lay down our lives
for each other.   *(1 Jn 3:16)*

ALL    Therefore, choose life.
Love alone renews life.
Live prepared to lose life.

READER    She who finds life
will lose her life,
and she who loses her life
for Jesus' sake
will find life everlasting.   *(Mt 10:39)*

ALL SING    Therefore, choose life.
Love alone renews life.
Live prepared to lose life.

READER    Nation will fight
against nation,

and kingdom
against kingdom.
Earthquakes
and plagues
and famines
will occur
and fearful signs
in the heavens.
Men will seize you
and persecute you,
and will hand you over
to prison
and bring you before tribunals
for judgement,
all because of my name.
This is your call
to bear witness,
so take these words to heart:
Do not prepare your defense,
for I myself
will give you eloquence
and wisdom
none can contradict.
You will be betrayed
by family and friends,
and some of you
will be put to death.
You will be hated
by all
because of my name,
but not a hair of your head
will perish.
Your endurance
will win you
your lives.   *(Lk 21:10-19)*

**LEADER**      *Perpetua* and *Felicitas*,
saints of third-century
Carthage,
heroic women,
martyrs
of the persecuted Church:

**ALL**      Hail, valiant women!
Your name is written in the book of life!

**LEADER**      *Joan of Arc*,
teenager who raised
the seige of Orleans and restored power
to the throne of France,
condemned by the Church's Inquisition,
burned at the stake as a heretic
in 1431,
canonized a saint in 1920,
the patron saint of France:

| ALL | Hail, valiant woman! |
| | Your name is written in the book of life! |
| | |
| LEADER | *Maura Clark, Ita Ford, Dorothy Kazel,* |
| | and *Jean Donovan,* |
| | Americans in mission, |
| | in 1980 |
| | martyrs of El Salvador: |
| | |
| ALL | Hail, valiant women! |
| | Your name is written in the book of life! |

## SILENT PRAYER

| READER | Greater love than this |
| | no woman has, |
| | than to lay down her life |
| | for her friends. *(Jn 15:13)* |
| | |
| LEADER | *Anaconda,* |
| | sixteenth century, |
| | American Indian warrior, |
| | who resisted the European invasion |
| | and exploitation |
| | of her people, |
| | was captured |
| | and executed: |
| | |
| ALL | Hail, valiant woman! |
| | Your name is written in the book of life! |
| | |
| LEADER | *Hannah Senesh,* |
| | Hungarian Jewish martyr, |
| | killed by the Nazis |
| | in 1944 |
| | after parachuting into Yugoslavia |
| | to warn Jews |
| | of the Holocaust: |
| | |
| ALL | Hail, valiant woman! |
| | Your name is written in the book of life! |
| | |
| LEADER | *Christa McAuliffe,* |
| | teacher and pioneer, |
| | America's first ordinary citizen |
| | in space, |
| | whom God received |
| | in a chariot of fire |
| | in 1986: |
| | |
| ALL | Hail, valiant woman! |
| | Your name is written in the book of life! |

## SILENT PRAYER

| READER | Do not fear those |
| | who kill the body. |
| | They cannot kill |
| | the soul. *(Mt 10:28)* |

| | Be faithful unto death,<br>and I will give you<br>the crown of life.  *(Rev 2:10)* |
|---|---|
| **LEADER** | *Mary Dyer*,<br>Quaker,<br>Massachusetts Bay,<br>hanged in 1660<br>in Boston<br>by the Church: |
| **ALL** | Hail, valiant woman!<br>Your name is written in the book of life! |
| **LEADER** | *Bridget Bishop*,<br>convicted of witchcraft<br>and hanged in Salem<br>in 1692: |
| **ALL** | Hail, valiant woman!<br>Your name is written in the book of life! |
| **LEADER** | *Anne Frank*,<br>young Jewish girl,<br>victim of the Holocaust<br>in 1945: |
| **ALL** | Hail, valiant woman!<br>Your name is written in the book of life! |

## SILENT PRAYER

| | |
|---|---|
| **READER** | Whatever you sow<br>has to die<br>before it is given new life.<br>What is sown<br>is perishable,<br>what is raised<br>is imperishable.<br>What is sown in dishonor,<br>is raised in glory.<br>What is sown in weakness,<br>is raised in power.  *(1 Cor 15:36,42-43)* |
| **LEADER** | All women destroyed by persecution,<br>whose bodies have been violated,<br>whose spirits have been humiliated,<br>who were imprisoned and put to death:<br><br>*Martyrs and saints of the early Church:* |
| **ALL** | Hail, valiant women!<br>Your names are written in the book of life! |
| **LEADER** | *Victims of the Inquisition—condemned as heretics<br>by the Church*: |
| **ALL** | Hail, valiant women!<br>Your names are written in the book of life! |

**LEADER**   *Victims of the Reformation—condemned as witches*
            *by the Church*:

**ALL**     Hail, valiant women!
            Your names are written in the book of life!

**LEADER**   *American Indian women—destroyed by our nation's*
            *ruthless expansion*:

**ALL**     Hail, valiant women!
            Your names are written in the book of life!

**LEADER**   *Black women slaves—destroyed by our nation's*
            *disdain for people of color*:

**ALL**     Hail, valiant women!
            Your names are written in the book of life!

**LEADER**   *Jewish women—destroyed by the Holocaust*
            *and by the world's indifference to the reality*
            *of the Holocaust*:

**ALL**     Hail, valiant women!
            Your names are written in the book of life!

**LEADER**   *Victims of genocide—Jews, Armenians,*
            *Ukrainians, Cambodians*:

**ALL**     Hail, valiant women!
            Your names are written in the book of life!

**LEADER**   *Victims of the violence of war—in*
            *Afghanistan, Ireland, Lebanon, El Salvador, Guatemala,*
            *Nicaragua, and in countless territorial*
            *and tribal disputes*:

**ALL**     Hail, valiant women!
            Your names are written in the book of life!

**LEADER**   *Victims of oppressive regimes—Chile, the Soviet Union,*
            *South Africa, Iran*:

**ALL**     Hail, valiant women!
            Your names are written in the book of life!

**LEADER**   *Victims of famine and drought, who died of*
            *hunger and thirst—in Ethiopia, the Sudan, and*
            *other impoverished nations*:

**ALL**     Hail, valiant women!
            Your names are written in the book of life!

**LEADER**   *Victims of patriarchal institutions—*
            *the government, business corporations, the Church*:

**ALL**     Hail, valiant women!
            Your names are written in the book of life!

**LEADER**   *Women who have died giving birth to new life:*

**ALL**     Hail, valiant women!
            Your names are written in the book of life!

| | |
|---|---|
| **VOICE** | We remember<br>all those heroines<br>whose names<br>are in the book of life,<br>and we call on them<br>for courage<br>in our own journey<br>of faith.<br>May they help us<br>know and understand<br>the purpose<br>of our lives<br>and the meaning<br>of this word: |
| **READER** | While we live<br>we are always<br>being given up to death<br>for Jesus' sake.　*(2 Cor 4:11)* |
| **VOICE** | Women especially understand<br>how giving shapes<br>what we receive,<br>how sharing blood<br>as the fetus forms,<br>spilling blood<br>for a higher cause,<br>means relinquishing life<br>as it always was<br>in exchange for life<br>as it was meant to be.<br>Death and life<br>go hand in hand:<br>this is woman's reality.<br>Women comprehend<br>what Jesus meant:<br>death is the consequence<br>of dissent. |
| **LEADER** | Let us reflect on the relationship of death<br>to life in our own lives and experience;<br>then let us share with one another<br>some of the ways we die,<br>as we struggle to give birth to life. |

## SILENT REFLECTION

## SHARED EXPERIENCE

| | |
|---|---|
| **VOICE** | Jesus said to Martha:<br>"I am the resurrection and the life."　*(Jn 11:25)* |
| **ALL** | The written code kills, but the Spirit gives life.<br><div align="right">*(2 Cor 3:6)*</div> |

| | |
|---|---|
| **VOICE** | Jesus says to all of his followers: "I am the resurrection and the life." |
| **ALL** | The written code kills, but the Spirit gives life. |
| **VOICE** | Jesus says to the institutional Church: "I am the resurrection and the life." |
| **ALL** | The written code kills, but the Spirit gives life. |
| **VOICE ONE** | El Shaddai, Shekinah, be the Soul of my sufficiency. |
| **VOICE TWO** | I will lift you up on eagles' wings, release within you silent springs. |
| **ALL** | Praise to You, life-giving Spirit! |
| **VOICE ONE** | Jesus, Hope of the vanquished, free my mind from the fears invading me. |
| **VOICE TWO** | In times of terror, I am there, when weapons of war are everywhere. |
| **ALL** | Praise to You, life-giving Spirit! |
| **VOICE ONE** | Spirit spiraling in, the Key to all of the courage alive in me. |
| **VOICE TWO** | I am the One to whom you belong, the pulsating silence within your song. |
| **ALL** | Praise to You, life-giving Spirit! |
| **LEADER** | Let us pray: |

## SILENT PRAYER

| | |
|---|---|
| **LEADER** | God of power, God of people, |

You are the life of all
that lives,
energy
that fills the earth,
vitality
that brings to birth,
the impetus
toward making whole
whatever is bruised
or broken.
In You we grow
to know the truth
that sets all creation free.
You are the song
the whole earth sings,
the promise
liberation brings,
now and forever.

**ALL**     Amen.

**ALL SING**     "You Are the Song" (See page 243.)

## BENEDICTION

**LEADER**     With wisdom and understanding,
with justice and mercy,
with courage and commitment,
may you (we) be blessed,
this day
and every day,
by the God who has loved us all
into life.

**ALL**     Give us life
according to Your promise;
give us life
according to Your justice;
give us life
according to Your word,
we pray! *(Ps 119:154,156)*

**LEADER**     Blessed be God forever!

**ALL**     Blessed be God forever!

**LEADER**     Let the people say:

**ALL**     Amen!

# TIME

*Underlying this community reflection on time is an awareness of the Eternal. Our body is driven by the clock, but not our soul or our spirit. An hourglass would be an appropriate symbol to set before the group, to remind all that our days are numbered and swiftly flow the years. To heighten a sense of timelessness, traditional Latin phrases constitute the community's response. However, words for "Christ" and "Lord" are written as feminine.*

> *Benedicamus Dominae.*
> Let us bless the One who reigns.
> *Ora pro nobis.*
> Pray for us.
> *Christa adveniat.*
> Let Christ come.
> *Magnificat anima mea Dominam!*
> My soul glorifies the One who reigns.

*Sit quietly, for a time, and focus your heart, before proceeding with the ritual.*

**VOICE ONE**  Once upon a time...

**VOICE TWO**  for a time,
and times,
and half a time...   *(Rev 12:14)*

**VOICE ONE**  when the lights had been fixed
in the firmament
to define the days
and the months
and the years...

**VOICE TWO**   and the seasons
were all established,
and morning
and evening
continued
as routinely as
ritual…

**VOICE ONE**   God created woman
and man,
made woman
intensely alive
to time,
with a sensitive,
sensual
sense of time…

**VOICE TWO**   instilled the recompense
of time
in her womb
and will
and reason,
replicated
within her
part of the primacy
of creation,
linked seasons of time
and timelessness
to the seasons
of her heart,
love's loveliest
variation.

**VOICE ONE**   For a time,
and times,
and half a time…

**VOICE TWO**   woman
interacts with time
intuitively,
inherently
whenever her Psychological Clock
beats with empathy:

**CHORUS/ALL** *Benedicamus Dominae.*
*Ora pro nobis.*

**READER**   "They have no wine,"
the woman said.
"Woman, what has that to do
with me?" said Jesus.
"My time
has not yet come." *(Jn 2:3-4)*

**VOICE ONE**  Blessed is she
who knows the time
and discerns
the place
for miracles,
for saving face.

**VOICE TWO**  Hail, full of grace!
Theotokos!
Through you,
with you,
in you
in time
is the fullness
of time,
Messiah
for all time,
suddenly
hear the news
now is the time:

**VOICE ONE**  *Christa
adveniat.*

**VOICE TWO**  *Christa!
Magnificat
anima mea
Dominam!*

**CHORUS/ALL** *Ora pro nobis!*

## SILENT REFLECTION

**VOICE ONE**  For a time,
and times,
and half a time...

**VOICE TWO**  woman
interacts with time
instinctively,
insistently,
whenever her Biological Clock
encounters viability:

**CHORUS/ALL** *Benedicamus Dominae.
Ora pro nobis.*

**READER**  A woman in labor
is apprehensive,
because her time
has come;
but when she has delivered,
her anguish is forgotten
in her joy for the child
that is born.   *(Jn 16:21)*

**VOICE ONE**    Like water
wearing away
a rock,
the body's biological
clock,
clearly conceiving
reality
in a monthly fling
with fertility,
is synchronous,
cyclical,
correlate
of earth's own tendency
to create:

**VOICE TWO**    and when ovarian time
is stilled,
its mandates
finally
fulfilled,
the throes of labor
linger.
Blessed the womb
that has conceived?
Rather,
blessed are they
who have believed.

**VOICE ONE**    *Christa
adveniat.*

**VOICE TWO**    *Christa!
Magnificat
anima mea
Dominam!*

**CHORUS/ALL** *Ora pro nobis!*

## SILENT REFLECTION

**VOICE ONE**    For a time,
and times,
and half a time…

**VOICE TWO**    woman
interacts with time
intentionally,
sequentially,
whenever her Logical Clock
reveals its capacity:

**CHORUS/ALL** *Benedicamus Dominae.
Ora pro nobis.*

**READER**    She finds her labor
well worth while,

her lamp burns through the night;
she does not neglect
her household,
for all are fed
and warmly clothed
under her management.   *(Prov 31:15,18,21,27)*

**VOICE ONE**   A woman's day
is never done,
from early dawn
to setting sun.

**VOICE TWO**   In Africa,
awake at five,
off to the fields where
to survive
she works the frugal earth
till three,
gathers firewood
rigorously,
carries it home,
sets it ablaze,
pounds cassava,
grinds the maize,
carries water from afar
on her head
in an earthen jar,
feeds her children,
feeds her man,
eats, then washes bowls
and pans
and children,
after a day like that,
she falls exhausted
on her mat.

**VOICE ONE**   Wherever she is situated
globally,
woman must function
efficiently;

**VOICE TWO**   domestically,
professionally,
so much more
of her time
and talent
and energy
must be
accounted for.

**VOICE ONE**   *Christa
adveniat.*

**VOICE TWO**   *Christa!*
*Magnificat*
*anima mea*
*Dominam!*

**CHORUS/ALL** *Ora pro nobis!*

## SILENT REFLECTION

**VOICE ONE**   For a time,
and times,
and half a time...

**VOICE TWO**   woman
interacts with time
internally,
with integrity,
whenever her Ontological Clock
champions serendipity:

**CHORUS/ALL** *Benedicamus Dominae.*
*Ora pro nobis.*

**READER**   There is a season
for everything,
a time for every purpose
under heaven.   *(Ecc 3:1)*

**VOICE ONE**   Stillness,
discernment,
affirming experience
at the start
of every deliberation
of the heart
is part of woman's
integrity.

**VOICE TWO**   What
at the essence
of all that lives
gives truth
its trustworthy
quality?
No code
nor creed,
no guarantee
other than
one's own reality:
spirit
is life.

**VOICE ONE**   *Christa*
*adveniat.*

**VOICE TWO**   *Christa!*
*Magnificat*
*anima mea*
*Dominam!*

**CHORUS/ALL** *Ora pro nobis!*

## SILENT REFLECTION

**VOICE ONE**   For a time,
and times,
and half a time...

**VOICE TWO**   woman
interacts with time
systemically,
inclusively,
whenever her Cosmological Clock
questions validity:

**CHORUS/ALL** *Benedicamus Dominae.*
*Ora pro nobis.*

**READER**   From the fig tree,
learn a lesson.
When the branch is in bud
and leaves appear,
summer is close at hand.   *(Mt 24:32)*

**VOICE ONE**   When orchards
abound
with grape
and fig
and vats overflow
with succulent juices
and barns are prepared
for a bountiful harvest,
remember
the barren
and bleak
December.

**VOICE TWO**   The poor
in spring
are poor
in the fall,
some have
so little,
some have it all;
one nation sows,
another reaps,
some pray for loans,
some play for keeps:
woe to you,
who horde away
survival
while people die
today.

**VOICE ONE**   *Christa*
*adveniat.*

**VOICE TWO**  *Christa!*
*Magnificat*
*anima mea*
*Dominam!*

**CHORUS/ALL** *Ora pro nobis!*

## SILENT REFLECTION

**VOICE ONE**  For a time,
and times,
and half a time...

**VOICE TWO**  woman
interacts with time
mystically,
wholistically,
whenever her Theological Clock
beats relentlessly:

**CHORUS/ALL** *Benedicamus Dominae.*
*Ora pro nobis.*

**READER**  The woman was given eagle's wings
that she might fly from the serpent
and flee into the wilderness,
to the place where she would be nourished
for a time, and times,
and half a time.
And the woman fled
into the wilderness,
to a place that had been prepared
by God,
a place where she would be nourished
for a time, and times,
and half a time.   *(Rev 12:6,14)*

**VOICE ONE**  Grace
and peace
to all who flee
because of their
vulnerability.

**VOICE TWO**  A place
of oasis,
of nourishing springs
awaits the one with
eagle's wings.

**VOICE ONE**  *Christa*
*adveniat.*

**VOICE TWO**  *Christa!*
*Magnificat*
*anima mea*
*Dominam!*

**CHORUS/ALL** *Ora pro nobis!*

## SILENT REFLECTION

**LEADER**      Let us take some time now
to sit with silence
and reflect on our own relationship
to time.
How do you feel about time?
What is your personal experience of time?
Time on your hands?
Running out of time?
Time for everything under the sun?
Think about time,
its possibilities
and its limitations,
and then share with one another
the fruit of that reflection.

## SILENT REFLECTION

## SHARED EXPERIENCE

**LEADER**      There's a season for everything
under the sun,
a time to do
and a time to be done,
a time to laugh
and a time to cry,
a time to live
and a time to die.

**SIDE ONE**    A time for dying and a time for rebirth.
**SIDE TWO**    A time for the spirit and a time for earth.

**SIDE ONE**    A time for laughter, a time for tears.
**SIDE TWO**    A time for courage and a time for fear.

**SIDE ONE**    A time to cling and a time to release.
**SIDE TWO**    A time for war and a time for peace.

**SIDE ONE**    A time to talk and a time to be still.
**SIDE TWO**    A time to care and time to kill.

**SIDE ONE**    A time alone. A time for romance.
**SIDE TWO**    A time to mourn. A time to dance.

**SIDE ONE**    A time to keep. A time to lose.
**SIDE TWO**    A time to be told. A time to choose.

**SIDE ONE**    A time to tear down. A time to rebuild.
**SIDE TWO**    A time to be empty. A time to be filled.

**SIDE ONE**    A time to welcome and to send away.
**SIDE TWO**    A time to complain and a time to pray.

| | |
|---|---|
| **SIDE ONE** | A time to share and a time to save. |
| **SIDE TWO** | A time to break rules. A time to behave. |
| **SIDE ONE** | A time to free and a time to bind. |
| **SIDE TWO** | A time to search and a time to find. |
| **SIDE ONE** | A time to plant and a time to uproot. |
| **SIDE TWO** | A time to be barren. A time to bear fruit. |
| **SIDE ONE** | A time of plenty. |
| **SIDE TWO** | A time of need. |
| **SIDE ONE** | A time to follow. |
| **SIDE TWO** | A time to lead. |
| **SIDE ONE** | A time to give. |
| **SIDE TWO** | A time to take. |
| **SIDE ONE** | A time to bend. |
| **SIDE TWO** | A time to break. |
| **SIDE ONE** | A time to hurt. |
| **SIDE TWO** | A time to heal. |
| **SIDE ONE** | A time for secrets. |
| **SIDE TWO** | A time to reveal. |
| **SIDE ONE** | A time to let go. |
| **SIDE TWO** | A time to hold. |
| **SIDE ONE** | A time to be young. |
| **SIDE TWO** | A time to grow old. |
| **SIDE ONE** | A time to rip open. |
| **SIDE TWO** | A time to mend. |
| **SIDE ONE** | A time to begin, |
| **SIDE TWO** | and a time to end. |

**LEADER**　There's a season for everything
under the sun,
a time to do
and a time to be done,
a time to laugh
and a time to cry,
a time to live
and a time to die.　*(Adapted from Ecc 3:1-8)*

**LEADER**　Let us pray:

## SILENT PRAYER

**LEADER**　Eternal God,
transcending time,
yet one with creation
conditioned by time,
You nurture within us
a hunger

for entering into
Your timelessness.
As we struggle
to redeem and renew
the times,
we await that day
in the fullness of time
when You will return
to gather us in
with justice
and mercy
and peace
forever.

**ALL**    Amen.

**ALL SING**    "Take the Time" (See page 245.)

## BENEDICTION

**LEADER**    The vision will be fulfilled
in its own time.
If it seems slow in coming,
wait for it,
for it will surely come.   *(Hab 2:3)*
And as you (we) wait,
may all things work together
for good,   *(Rm 8:28)*
may you (we) be blessed
with wisdom
and discernment
and determination
and patience,
may you (we) take the time
to grow in grace
day by day.

**ALL**    Amen.

# CIRCLE OF LOVE

*Set up chairs to form two concentric circles that face each other. The inner circle should face outward and the outer circle should face inward. When it is time for the ritual to begin, invite people to take their places and to enter into silence. The room should be bathed in the warm glow of a whole array of candles. Savor the stillness, and begin.*

**LEADER**    The circle of love
is repeatedly broken
because of the sin
of exclusion.
We create separate circles:
the inner circle
and the outer circle,
the circle of power
and the circle of despair,
the circle of privilege
and the circle of deprivation.
We carefully define our circles,
at work
or at worship,
with family
and with friends,
peripheral
or very special,
and function,
not always willingly,
within their parameters.
   *(Pause)*

Some circles nourish,
other circles destroy.
The circle of fifths
is the cornerstone
of much of the world's music.
The cycle of poverty
excludes whole populations
from the necessities of life.
Time itself is cyclical,
spiraling through aeons
and galaxies
seemingly without end;
yet as each season rolls around,
we are all a little older,
some are a little wiser,
none of us is unchanged.
*(Pause)*

The circle of love
is broken,
whenever there is alienation,
whenever there is misunderstanding,
whenever there is insensitivity
and a hardening of the heart.
The circle of love
is broken,
whenever we cannot see eye to eye,
whenever we cannot link hand to hand,
whenever we cannot live heart to heart
and affirm our differences.
*(Pause)*

Before we can pray,
before we can dream,
before we can witness
to justice and peace,
we must be a single circle,
a single, unbroken circle,
a wide open, welcoming circle.
Let us build this circle of love.

### A CIRCLE OF LOVE

**LEADER**     Let us ask forgiveness
for the many times
we have severed the circle
of love,
by word
or deed
or attitude.

**INNER CIRCLE**

We ask forgiveness
of one another,
woman to woman,
sister to sister.

**OUTER CIRCLE**

We ask forgiveness
of one another,
as children of God,
as friend to friend.

**INNER CIRCLE**

Too many times
have we failed to stand
together
in solidarity.

**OUTER CIRCLE**

Too many times
have we judged one another,
condemning those things
we did not understand.

**INNER CIRCLE**

We ask forgiveness
for assuming we know
all there is to know
about each other,
for presuming to speak
for each other,
for defining,
confining,
claiming,
naming,
limiting,
labeling,
conditioning,
interpreting,
and consequently oppressing
each other.

**OUTER CIRCLE**

We ask forgiveness
for making rules
based on private revelation,
for publicly condemning anyone
who fails to abide by them,
for imposing heavy penalties,
for excluding,
withholding,
insisting,
resisting
the inclusiveness of grace.
*(Pause)*

*The Leader invites the community to stand for the following prayer and blessing.*

**LEADER**      For the times we have hurt one another, we pray:

**ALL**      Forgive us our sins,
as we forgive all who have sinned against us.

**LEADER**      For the times we have hindered one another, we pray:

**ALL**      Forgive us our sins,
as we forgive all who have sinned against us.

**LEADER**      For the times we have scandalized one another, we pray:

**ALL**      Forgive us our sins,
as we forgive all who have sinned against us.

**LEADER**      Through God's grace
we are forgiven,
by the mercy of Shaddai,
through the love of the Christ,
in the power of the Spirit.
Let us rejoice and be glad.

**ALL**      Amen.

**LEADER**      As a sign of our forgiving,
let us greet each other
with a gesture of peace,
a peace that we wholeheartedly offer,
the peace that comes from God.

*After the exchange of peace, all return to their places.*

**LEADER**      As a sign of our having been forgiven,
let us come out of our separate circles
and form one circle of love.

*The Leader invites the community to rearrange the chairs into a single circle, facing in, and to stand in front of the chairs.*

**LEADER**      Lift up your hearts to the One Holy God.

**ALL**      We lift up our hearts to the One Holy God.

**LEADER**      Open yourselves to be touched by Her word.

**ALL**      We open ourselves to be touched by Her word.

**LEADER**      Surrender yourselves to Her presence within.

**ALL**      We surrender ourselves to Her presence within.

**READER**      We are a chosen people,
united in our vocation.
When we stand together,
we are the new creation.
Holy the spirit that binds us.
Holy our shared liberation.

| | |
|---|---|
| **LEADER** | Holy the God predisposed to forgive. |
| **ALL** | Holy the God-given lives that we live. |
| **LEADER** | Holy the Word that proclaims the Good News. |
| **ALL** | Holy the Gospel too good to refuse. |
| **LEADER** | Holy the Lamp that enlightens our way. |
| **ALL** | Holy the Praise in the prayers that we pray. |
| **LEADER** | Holy the Vision enticing us on. |
| **ALL** | Holy the Hope it is founded upon. |
| **LEADER** | Holy the Wisdom on which we depend. |
| **ALL** | Holy the Waiting for suffering to end. |
| **LEADER** | Holy the Heart that we know understands. |
| **ALL** | Holy the Spirit-led work of our hands. |
| **LEADER** | Holy the Love, may it ever increase. |
| **ALL** | Holy our striving for justice and peace. |
| **ALL SING** | "Circle of Love" (See page 247.) |

*The Leader invites all to be seated.*

## SECOND SPIRAL

**READER**     Imagine a circle,
and in its midst
a center,
and from this center
rays extend;
each one,
each radius
radiates
from the center
of the circle.
The farther these radii
extend from the center,
the more they diverge,
the more remote
they become from one another.
On the other hand,
as they approach the center,
they converge
and come together.
Now imagine that this circle
is the world,
and the center of the circle
is God,
and the radii from center
to circumference,

from the innermost point
to the outer edge,
and from the outer edge
to the very center,
are the paths of life
of people.
When people withdraw
from the center,
from God,
they withdraw from one another,
and when they approach the center,
when they seek after God,
they come closer to one another.
Such is the circle of love.
If we do not love,
if we are distant from God,
we are distant from one another.
When we love God,
when we are one with God,
we are one in our love of each other.
The converse is also true.
The closer we are to each other,
the closer we are to God.
Such is the circle of love.

*(Based on a text by Abba Dorotheus,*
*seventh-century Eastern Orthodox mystic)*

## SILENT REFLECTION

**LEADER**     God invites us to extend
our circle of love
beyond the circle of women.
God asks us to include
those with whom
it is hard to be reconciled.
And so we pray:

Mother of Mercy,
You hold us all
in Your reconciling arms.
Help us to forgive
those who perpetuate
the patriarchal system,
who foster misogynist values,
excluding us
from sacred spaces,
patronizing us
in professional places,
who monopolize
and abuse power,
pushing us toward despair.
Help us forgive

those who have abused
our bodies and our spirits
and trampled on our souls.
As we condemn
systemic evil,
may we embrace
both oppressed
and oppressor
in our widening circle
of love,
and may we love one another
as You love us,
now and always.

**ALL**   Amen.

**ALL SING**  "Circle of Love" (Refrain only, see page 247.)

### THIRD SPIRAL

**READER**  The Indian's symbol is the circle, the hoop.
Nature wants things to be round.
The bodies of human beings and animals
have no corners.
With us the circle stands
for the togetherness of people
who sit with one another
around the campfire,
relatives and friends united in peace
while the pipe passes from hand to hand.
The camp in which every tipi had its place
was also in a ring.
The tipi was a ring in which people sat in a circle
and all families in the village
were in turn circles
within a larger circle,
part of the larger hoop
which was the seven campfires of the Sioux,
representing one nation.
The nation was only part of the universe,
in itself circular and made of the earth,
which is round,
of the sun which is round,
of the stars which are round.
The moon, the horizon, the rainbow -
circles within circles,
with no beginning and no end. *(John Fire/Lame Deer)*

## SILENT REFLECTION

**LEADER**  God invites us to extend
our circle of love
beyond all human boundaries.

Let us open our hearts
to embrace all people
of every color
and every culture;
and animals,
and the earth,
and the galaxies of the universe.
Welcome to our circle of love!

**ALL SING**    "Circle of Love" (Refrain only, see page 247.)

**LEADER**    Let us pray:

We give thanks
that we are all part
of the family circle of God,
forgiving one another,
loving one another
because God has first loved us,
that God's Spirit
has banished distinctions
between Jew and Greek,
between slave and free,
between female and male,
between those who are in power
and those who are powerless.
We give thanks
that we are one
in the love of the One
who loves in us,
forever and ever.

**ALL**    Amen.

## BENEDICTION

**LEADER**    May God bless us,
embrace us,
and send us forth
renewed,
refreshed,
revitalized.
May we live each day
in the name of Love,
and include all
in our circle of love,
and treat all
with a spirit of love,
through the Spirit
who is Love.

**ALL**    Amen.

**SONG**    "Circle of Love" (See page 247.)

# SING OF A BLESSING

*Arrange chairs in a circle. In the center of the circle,on a small table, place a bottle of wine (or an appropriate substitute) and a cup or chalice, the Cup of Blessing. In preparation, rehearse the music and the dance to "Blessing Song" (pages 251 and 202). Stand for the opening praise.*

## PRAISE AND THANKSGIVING

| | |
|---|---|
| **LEADER** | Blessed be God! |
| **ALL** | Blessed be God! |
| **LEADER** | Blessed be Her holy Name! |
| **ALL** | Blessed be Her holy Name! |
| **LEADER** | Blessed be Jesus, truly God and truly human! |
| **ALL** | Blessed be Jesus, truly God and truly human! |
| **LEADER** | Blessed be the name of Jesus! |
| **ALL** | Blessed be the name of Jesus! |
| **LEADER** | Blessed be His compassionate heart! |
| **ALL** | Blessed be His compassionate heart! |
| **LEADER** | Blessed be the Word-made-flesh in the world! |
| **ALL** | Blessed be the Word-made-flesh in the world! |
| **LEADER** | Blessed be God-with-us-always! |
| **ALL** | Blessed be God-with-us-always! |
| **LEADER** | Blessed is the earth and all its people! |
| **ALL** | Blessed is the earth and all its people! |
| **LEADER** | Blessed is the Church, the communion of saints! |
| **ALL** | Blessed is the Church, the communion of saints! |

| | |
|---|---|
| **LEADER** | Blessed is our striving for unity and peace! |
| **ALL** | Blessed is our striving for unity and peace! |
| **LEADER** | For all our blessings, we give thanks and praise. |
| **ALL** | For all our blessings, we give thanks and praise. |
| **ALL SING** | "We Are the Church" (See page 249.) |

## PRAYER

| | |
|---|---|
| **LEADER** | Our Mother, our Father... |
| **ALL** | All-merciful, Almighty... |
| **LEADER** | who inspired our forefathers in all<br>they achieved, |
| **ALL** | who consoled our foremothers for all<br>they were denied, |
| **LEADER** | blessed is Your power among us, |
| **ALL** | blessed is Your presence within. |
| **LEADER** | May we freely and faithfully preach Your word, |
| **ALL** | and translate that word into visible deeds, |
| **LEADER** | deeds of justice, |
| **ALL** | and deeds of mercy, |
| **LEADER** | feeding and sheltering, |
| **ALL** | witnessing to peace. |
| **LEADER** | Help us to follow the right path. |
| **ALL** | Shape our spirit with Your Holy Spirit, |
| **LEADER** | a spirit of wisdom and compassion, |
| **ALL** | an abiding hunger for truth. |
| **LEADER** | Bless all ministers, clergy and lay, |
| **ALL** | and our many ministries, ordained and unordained. |
| **LEADER** | Hasten the day when all are equally valued, |
| **ALL** | and true mutuality is a hallmark of the Church. |
| **LEADER** | God of all people, |
| **ALL** | of women as well as men, |
| **LEADER** | as You stand by our brothers who are committed to change, |
| **ALL** | as You strengthen our sisters whose vision<br>brings hope, |
| **LEADER** | we praise You, |
| **ALL** | we bless You<br>we sing of Your glory. |
| **LEADER** | Blessed be God,<br>Source of all blessings,<br>who makes of us<br>a blessing<br>through Her Spirit<br>within us,<br>Her presence |

around us,
now and forever.

**ALL**        Amen!
Blessing and glory
and wisdom and thanksgiving
and honor and power
and strength to our God
forever and ever!
Amen!   *(Rev 7:12)*

## THE BEATITUDES: REFLECTION AND PRAYER

**LEADER**    Let us enter
into the spirit of the Beatitudes,
and more deeply into the presence of Jesus,
as we reflect on his teaching
from the Sermon on the Mount.
Listen as each Beatitude is announced.
Take time to reflect on its meaning.
Call to mind persons, issues,
or significant concerns
related to its theme.
Then during the time of sharing
that follows our reflecting,
voice your concerns within the group,
so that we might hold them up in prayer.

**READER**    Blessed are the poor in spirit,
for theirs is the household of heaven.   *(Mt 5:3)*

## SILENT REFLECTION

## SHARED REFLECTIONS

**LEADER**    All the poor,
in reality
and in spirit,
we lift to God
in prayer.
For the people
and the concerns
that were mentioned here
we ask a special blessing,
and for ourselves
the grace to be truly poor
in spirit.

**ALL**        Amen.

**READER**    Blessed are all who mourn,
for they shall be comforted.  *(Mt 5:4)*

## SILENT REFLECTION

## SHARED REFLECTIONS

**LEADER** For all who weep,
for all who mourn,
we ask a special blessing,
and for ourselves,
we ask for the grace
to comfort
and console.
Come, Holy Spirit,
Comforter,
now and forever.

**ALL** Amen.

**READER** Blessed are the gentle,
for they shall inherit the earth.  *(Mt 5:5)*

## SILENT REFLECTION

## SHARED REFLECTIONS

**LEADER** For the gentle,
the meek,
the lowly,
all who are long-suffering,
patient,
unsure,
we ask a special blessing,
and for ourselves
we ask for the grace
not to take ourselves too seriously,
we who were fashioned
from mud and clay
by God our Creator.

**ALL** Amen.

**READER** Blessed are all who hunger and thirst for justice,
for they shall be satisfied.  *(Mt 5:6)*

## SILENT REFLECTION

## SHARED REFLECTIONS

**LEADER** For all who hunger
and thirst
for justice,
for all who hunger
and thirst,
for victims
of the injustice
of oppression
and all who work
for their liberation,

we ask a special blessing,
and for ourselves,
we ask for the grace
to be less
self-satisfied,
less comfortable with our abundance
while so many
are in need,
more inclined
to share our blessings
through Jesus,
the justice of God.

**ALL**    Amen.

**READER**    Blessed are the merciful,
for they shall be shown mercy.  *(Mt 5:7)*

## SILENT REFLECTION

## SHARED REFLECTIONS

**LEADER**    For all who have
forgiven others
for injury
done to themselves,
we ask a special blessing,
and for ourselves,
the grace to be forgiving,
generous,
merciful,
as our God is merciful
to us,
today and every day.

**ALL**    Amen.

**READER**    Blessed are the pure in heart,
for they shall see God.  *(Mt 5:8)*

## SILENT REFLECTION

## SHARED REFLECTIONS

**LEADER**    For all who are
clean of heart,
single-minded,
without guile,
we ask a special blessing,
and for ourselves,
we ask for the grace
of greater integrity,
that we might follow Jesus
in preaching the Gospel
faithfully
with our lives.

| | |
|---|---|
| **ALL** | Amen. |
| **READER** | Blessed are the peacemakers,<br>for they shall be called children of God.   *(Mt 5:9)* |

## SILENT REFLECTION

## SHARED REFLECTIONS

| | |
|---|---|
| **LEADER** | For all who<br>lay down their lives<br>for peace,<br>for all who<br>abandon their weapons<br>for peace,<br>for all who are radically committed<br>to peace,<br>we ask a special blessing,<br>and for ourselves,<br>the courage of our convictions<br>and an end<br>to the games of war,<br>through Jesus,<br>Peacemaker and<br>Peacekeeper,<br>to whom we say: |
| **ALL** | Amen! |
| **READER** | Blessed are all who are persecuted<br>for the cause of justice,<br>for theirs is the household of heaven.   *(Mt 5:10)* |

## SILENT REFLECTION

## SHARED REFLECTIONS

| | |
|---|---|
| **LEADER** | For all who endure<br>persecution<br>to further the cause<br>of justice,<br>for all who are<br>innocent victims,<br>we ask a special blessing,<br>and for ourselves,<br>the grace to speak out<br>for what is right<br>and to take a public stand<br>whenever injustice threatens,<br>at home or abroad,<br>for this we pray. |
| **ALL** | Amen. |

# THE CUP OF BLESSING

*The Leader lifts up the Cup of Blessing and prays:*

**LEADER**    We thank You,
God our Creator,
for all the blessings
of the universe,
for the blessings
of our tradition:
the Gospel,
the community,
our faith.
For all of the blessings
this cup represents,
the life within,
the love poured out,
the promises of Christ,
we give You thanks
and praise,
forever and ever.

**ALL**    Amen.

## THANKSGIVING FOR INDIVIDUAL BLESSINGS

**LEADER**    Let us now
give thanks
for specific blessings
we ourselves have received:

*The Leader begins by holding the Cup and giving thanks aloud for a specific blessing received, using the suggested sentence:*

**LEADER**    Thank you, God, for _____.

**ALL**    Thanks be to God!

*As the specific blessing is mentioned aloud, a community representative (Minister) pours a little wine from the bottle into the Cup of Blessing to symbolize the pouring of the individual's blessing into the Cup.*

*The Leader passes the Cup to the left, so it moves from person to person clockwise around the circle. As each person gives thanks for a particular blessing, the Minister pours a little wine into the Cup, and the community responds:*

Thanks be to God!

*When all have given thanks, the Minister is seated and the Cup of Blessing is returned to the Leader, who holds it, and prays:*

**LEADER**    The Cup of Blessing
which we bless

is our participation
in the covenant of Christ.   *(1 Cor 10:16)*
Let us drink then
a blessing
to one another
and a blessing
to the world.

## SHARING THE CUP OF BLESSING

*Again the Cup is passed from right to left around the circle. Each person drinks from the Cup in a silent, solemn, symbolic acceptance of all the blessings it contains.*

## THE CIRCLE OF BLESSING

## ALL SING/DANCE
"Blessing Song" (See pages 251 and 202.)

May the blessing of God go before you.
May Her grace and peace abound.
May Her Spirit live within you.
May Her love wrap you 'round.
May Her blessing remain with you always.
May you walk on holy ground.

# THE BLESSINGS OF THE UNIVERSE

**LEADER**   We give thanks for the power
inherent in
the symbols to which we lay claim:
the power of the Cup of Blessing
which holds all our hopes within it,
the power of the circle
which is love without discrimination,
which is life without an end,
the power of the center
who is Jesus
who is the Christ.
We call now on the Spirit of God
whose presence fills the universe,
who blesses us
and empowers us
to renew the face of the earth.

# PRAYER OF THE SIX DIRECTIONS

*During this prayer, turn bodily as a group toward each of the four compass directions; raise both arms high and look to the heavens when that direction is invoked; bend down and touch the ground when addressing the Spirit of earth.*

**LEADER**   We turn to the West for a blessing,
to the Spirit of Shalom:
make us whole, make us holy,

help us to love You
and one another
with our whole heart,
our whole mind,
our whole soul,
we pray:

**ALL**        Empower us, Holy Spirit!

**LEADER**    We turn to the North for a blessing,
to the Spirit of Integrity:
give us Your strength
and the courage to endure,
we pray:

**ALL**        Empower us, Holy Spirit!

**LEADER**    We turn to the East for a blessing,
to the Spirit of Illumination:
open our eyes to the sacredness
of every living thing,
we pray:

**ALL**        Empower us, Holy Spirit!

**LEADER**    We turn to the South for a blessing,
to the Spirit of Transformation:
help us to grow in wisdom
and grace
and the goodness of the ages,
we pray:

**ALL**        Empower us, Holy Spirit!

**LEADER**    We look to the Heavens for a blessing,
to the Spirit of Openness:
fill us with the wideness
of Your mercy
that lovingly embraces all,
we pray:

**ALL**        Empower us, Holy Spirit!

**LEADER**    We touch the Earth for a blessing,
and thereby touch the Spirit Incarnate
among us and
within us:
help us to be more human
and to praise You
through the work of our hands,
we pray:

**ALL**        Empower us, Holy Spirit!

## BENEDICTION

**LEADER**    Let us go forth from here
blessed and renewed

in the Spirit of Shalom,
the Spirit of Integrity,
the Spirit of Illumination,
the Spirit of Transformation,
with hopes lifted heavenward,
with hearts loving the earth,
in the name of our
creating,
liberating,
nurturing God.

**ALL**     Amen.

**SONG**     "Sing of A Blessing" (See page 252.)

# BLESSING SONG

## The Dance

*Rehearse the following dance movements before the beginning of the ritual. Dance prayers work best when the song is taught first, then the gestures, and then both are put together. Repetition is important for a feeling of ease, connection, and prayer to develop.*

OPENING POSITION The dance is performed with partners, either in two concentric circles, facing each other, or, if the space is crowded, with couples situated at random around the room. In either case, it is essential that all move in the same counterclockwise direction.

*May the blessing of God go before you.*

All face their partners. Hands are lightly joined. The hands rise, and with a continuous motion, as partners turn away from each other toward the counterclockwise line of direction, the outer hands of each pair disengage and the outer arm of each person arches upward and forward. Everyone is now facing her or his hand that is extended forward, "blessing" the way. (It feels more like a blessing if the wrist is tilted slightly upward, with the palm facing out.) Partners are holding inside hands.

*May Her grace and peace abound.*

Moving as a unit, with the "blessing" hand held in front, all take four steps forward, in the counterclockwise direction.

*May Her spirit live within you.*

Each person takes four more steps, making a complete circle around himself or herself, turning away from their partners, either to the left or to the right. This is accomplished with both arms extended, with a sense of blessing the area while turning. The movement is finished with partners facing each other, joining their hands together, at about waist height, affirming the spirit within one another.

*May Her love wrap you 'round.*

Hands are raised in unison, and then fan open overhead, lowering in an open embrace.

*May Her blessing remain with you always.*

Right elbows are linked, arms lifting upward, both arms held high in a folklike position. Partners take four steps circling around one another, clockwise, each person coming back to her or his original side, and facing counterclockwise.

*May you walk on holy ground.*

Walking side by side, with hands in the prayer position (palms together, fingertips pointing upward), partners take four steps forward counterclockwise. Each step is an expression of peace.

CONCLUSION After repeating the dance as many times as feels right for the ritual, ask all to face the center. The song is sung one more time, while all slowly raise both hands forward and upward in a blessing (palms face outward). On the last line *(may you walk on holy ground)* all bow, with palms together, held in front of the body. You are bowing to the God within each person.

*Choreography by Carla DeSola*
*Omega Liturgical Dance Company*

# SONGS

# MOTHER AND GOD

Mother and God, to You we sing:
wide is Your womb, warm is Your wing.
In You we live, move, and are fed,
sweet, flowing milk, life-giving bread.
Mother and God, to You we bring
all broken hearts, all broken wings.


Miriam Therese Winter
Copyright © Medical Mission Sisters, 1987

# MOTHER AND GOD

*Words and music by*
*Miriam Therese Winter*

Moth - er and God, to You we sing:
wide is Your womb, warm is Your wing.
In You we live, move, and are fed,
sweet, flow - ing milk, life - giv - ing bread.
Moth - er and God, to You we bring
all bro - ken hearts, all bro - ken wings.

# MOTHER EARTH

> Mother earth, sister sea,
> giving birth, energy,
> reaching out, touching me lovingly.

Formed from earth's own flesh and bone,
one with silt and sand and stone.

> Mother earth, sister sea,
> giving birth, energy,
> reaching out, touching me lovingly.

From the primal womb, we are
called to kinship with the stars.

> Mother earth, sister sea,
> giving birth, energy,
> reaching out, touching me lovingly.

With the rain we mingle tears,
to the winds we toss the years.

> Mother earth, sister sea,
> giving birth, energy,
> reaching out, touching me lovingly.

As our lives are flowering,
all the cosmic voices sing.

> Mother earth, sister sea,
> giving birth, energy,
> reaching out, touching me lovingly.

Blessed be God, Her woman's touch
gives us earth, who gives so much.

> Mother earth, sister sea,
> giving birth, energy,
> reaching out, touching me lovingly.

Miriam Therese Winter
Copyright © Medical Mission Sisters, 1987

# MOTHER EARTH

Words and music by
Miriam Therese Winter

**Refrain** ♩ = 96

E  F♯m  E  F♯m  E  C♯m

Moth - er earth,   sis - ter sea,   giv - ing birth,   en - er - gy,

F♯m  B7  E  *Fine*  2

reach - ing out,   touch - ing me   lov - ing - ly.

**Verses**

E9  E  C♯m  F♯m  B7  E

| Formed | from | earth's | own | flesh | and | bone, |
| From | the | pri - mal | womb, | we | | are |
| With | the | rain | we | min - gle | | tears, |
| As | our | lives | are | flow - er - | | ing, |
| Blessed | be | God, | Her | wom - an's | | touch |

A  E  F♯m  C♯m/G♯  B7  E  3

| one | with | silt | and | sand | and | stone. |
| called | to | kin - ship | with | the | | stars. |
| to | the | winds | we | toss | the | years. |
| all | the | cos - mic | voic - es | | | sing. |
| gives | us | earth, | who | gives | so | much. |

# BREATH OF GOD

Blow through me, Breath of God,
blow through me,
like a pipe, like a flute, like a reed,
making melody,
the cosmic song in me,
Breath of God.

# BREATH OF GOD

*Words and music by*
*Miriam Therese Winter*

Blow through me, Breath of God,

blow through me, like a

pipe, like a flute, like a reed, mak - ing mel - o - dy,

the cos - mic song in me, Breath of God.

# LIVING WATER

All who thirst for Living Water,
Cool and cleanse, Un-
Living Water, Living Water,
turn to You, Unfailing Spring. Wash our wounds and
failing Spring, cool and
Living Water, Living Spring; cool and comfort,
cleanse our spirits, Source of Life for ev'rything.
comfort ev'rything.
cool and comfort, cool and comfort ev'rything.

# YOU, GOD, ARE MY FIRMAMENT

You, God, are my firmament,
roof for my head, shelter from storm,
nourishing bread, tender and warm.

I will give thanks, I will sing praise,
with all of my heart, all of my days.

You, God, are a tower of strength.
I shall not fear, I shall not fall,
knowing You're near, guardian of all.

I will give thanks, I will sing praise,
with all of my heart, all of my days.

You, God, are my guiding light,
beacon from birth, helping to see,
lighting the earth, enlightening me.

I will give thanks, I will sing praise,
with all of my heart, all of my days.

Miriam Therese Winter
Copyright © Medical Mission Sisters, 1982

# YOU, GOD, ARE MY FIRMAMENT

Words and music by
Miriam Therese Winter

# MYSTERY

When I stand on a rolling hill and I look out to the sea,
I can feel the force of freedom finding fellowship with me.
I can hear a call to courage to be all that I might be.
Then I know I have known Mystery.

> It's the song of the universe, as the aeons fall away.
> It's the song that the stars sing and all the planets play.
> It's a song to the Power neither you nor I can see.
> It's a song to the One who is Mystery.

When I walk through a wooded grove to admire nature's art,
I can feel her weave her wisdom on the webbing of my heart.
I can hear her invitation to be part of all I see.
Then I know I have known Mystery.

> It's the song of the universe, as the aeons fall away.
> It's the song that the stars sing and all the planets play.
> It's a song to the Power neither you nor I can see.
> It's a song to the One who is Mystery.

As I run through the sunlight and the shadows of the years,
I can feel a strong sensation through the silence of the spheres.
I can hear a call to loving all, to immortality.
Then I know I have known Mystery.

> It's the song of the universe, as the aeons fall away.
> It's the song that the stars sing and all the planets play.
> It's a song to the Power neither you nor I can see.
> It's a song to the One who is Mystery.

Miriam Therese Winter
Copyright © Medical Mission Sisters, 1987

## MYSTERY

*Words and music by*
*Miriam Therese Winter*

freedom finding fellowship with me. I can
wisdom on the webbing of my heart. I can
sation through the silence of the spheres. I can

hear a call to courage to be all that I might be.
hear her invitation to be part of all I see.
hear a call to loving all, to immortality.

Then I know I have known Mystery.
Then I know I have known Mystery.
Then I know I have known Mystery.

*Refrain*

It's the 'song of the universe, as the aeons fall away. It's the song that the stars sing and all the planets play. It's a song to the Power neither you nor I can see. It's a song to the One who is Mystery.

# MAGNIFICAT

My soul gives glory to my God.
My heart pours out its praise.
God lifted up my lowliness
in many marvelous ways.

My God has done great things for me:
Holy is Her Name.
All people will declare me blessed,
and blessings they shall claim.

From age to age, to all who fear,
such mercy Love imparts,
dispensing justice far and near,
dismissing selfish hearts.

Love casts the mighty from their thrones,
promotes the insecure,
leaves hungry spirits satisfied,
the rich seem suddenly poor.

Praise God, whose loving Covenant
supports those in distress,
remembering past promises
with present faithfulness.


Text: Miriam Therese Winter
Copyright © Medical Mission Sisters, 1978, 1987

# MAGNIFICAT

*Words by*
*Miriam Therese Winter*

*Melody from*
*Wyeth's Repository of Sacred Music*

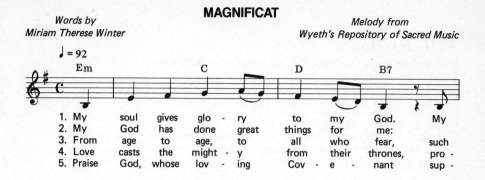

1. My soul gives glo - ry to my God. My
2. My God has done great things for me:
3. From age to age, to all who fear, such
4. Love casts the might - y from their thrones, pro -
5. Praise God, whose lov - ing Cov - e - nant sup -

heart pours out its praise. God lift - ed up my
Ho - ly is Her Name. All peo - ple will de -
mer - cy Love im - parts, dis - pens - ing jus - tice
motes the in - se - cure, leaves hun - gry spir - its
ports those in dis - tress, re - mem - ber - ing past

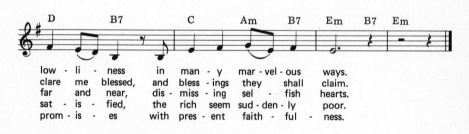

low - li - ness in man - y mar - vel - ous ways.
clare me blessed, and bless - ings they shall claim.
far and near, dis - miss - ing sel - fish hearts.
sat - is - fied, the rich seem sud - den - ly poor.
prom - is - es with pres - ent faith - ful - ness.

# THE VISIT

She walked in the summer through the heat on the hill.
She hurried as one who went with a will.
She danced in the sunlight when the day was done.
Her heart knew no evening, who carried the sun.

Fresh as a flower at the first ray of dawn,
she came to her cousin whose morning was gone.
There leaped a little child in the ancient womb,
and there leaped a little hope in every ancient tomb.

Hail, little sister, who heralds the spring.
Hail, brave mother, of whom prophets sing.
Hail to the moment beneath your breast.
May all generations call you blessed.

When you walk in the summer through the heat on the hill,
when you're wound with the wind and one with Her will,
be brave with the burden you are blessed to bear,
for it's Christ that you carry everywhere, everywhere, everywhere.


Miriam Therese Winter

# THE VISIT

*Words and music by*
*Miriam Therese Winter*

♩ = 116

1. She walked in the sum - mer through the
2. Fresh as a flow - er at the
3. Hail, lit - tle sis - ter, who
4. walk in the sum - mer through the

heat on the hill. She hur - ried as one who
first ray of dawn, she came to her cous-in whose
her - alds the spring. Hail, brave moth-er, of
heat on the hill, when you're wound with the wind and

went with a will. She danced in the sun - light when the
morn - ing was gone. There leaped a lit - tle child in the
whom proph-ets sing. Hail to the mo - ment be -
one with Her will, be brave with the bur - den you are

*Last time to Coda*

day was done. Her heart knew no eve - ning, who
an - cient womb, and there leaped a lit - tle hope in ev - 'ry
neath your breast. May all gen - er - a - tions
blessed to bear, for it's Christ that you car - ry ev - 'ry -

car - ried the sun.
an - cient tomb.
call you blessed.

4. When you

*Coda*

where, ev - 'ry - where, ev - 'ry - where.

# THANK YOU, GOD

Thank You, God, for the gift of birth,
for love made flesh to refresh the earth.
For life and strength and length of days,
we give You thanks and praise.

Love, You possessed me from the very start,
kept for Yourself my unsuspecting heart.

Thank You, God, for the gift of birth,
for love made flesh to refresh the earth.
For life and strength and length of days,
we give You thanks and praise.

Your grace discovers me when my heart hides.
If I should run from You, Your love abides.

Thank You, God, for the gift of birth,
for love made flesh to refresh the earth.
For life and strength and length of days,
we give You thanks and praise.

Love, You created me for wanting You.
May You remember me my whole life through.

Thank You, God, for the gift of birth,
for love made flesh to refresh the earth.
For life and strength and length of days,
we give You thanks and praise.

Miriam Therese Winter
Copyright © Medical Mission Sisters, 1978, 1982

# THANK YOU, GOD

Words and music by
Miriam Therese Winter

♩ = 104

Refrain

Thank You, God, for the gift of birth, for love made flesh to re-fresh the earth. For life and strength and length of days, we give You thanks and praise.

Verses

Love, You pos - sessed me from the ver - y start,
Your grace dis - cov - ers me when my heart hides.
Love, You cre - a - ted me for want - ing You.

kept for Your - self my un - sus - pect - ing heart.
If I should run from You, Your love a - bides.
May You re - mem - ber me my whole life through.

# WE ARE THE WORD

Mountains and meadows and free-flowing streams,
gardens and ghettoes and poor people's dreams,
down through the ages the good news is heard:
each of life's pages expresses the Word,
love that engages enfleshes the Word.

> Faith moves mountains, transcending creeds.
> The Word within words is embodied in deeds.
> Fear for the future finds hope in the past,
> for love was the first word, it's surely the last.

Mountains and meadows and free-flowing streams,
gardens and ghettoes and poor people's dreams,
down through the ages the good news is heard:
each of life's pages expresses the Word,
love that engages enfleshes the Word.

> The poor will have priv'lege, the hungry will eat.
> All of the homeless will dance in the street.
> In God's revelation, real love will release
> the reincarnation of justice and peace.

Mountains and meadows and free-flowing streams,
gardens and ghettoes and poor people's dreams,
down through the ages the good news is heard:
each of life's pages expresses the Word,
love that engages enfleshes the Word.

Miriam Therese Winter

# WE ARE THE WORD

Words and music by
Miriam Therese Winter

Moun - tains and mead - ows and free - flow - ing streams,
gar-dens and ghet-toes and poor peo-ple's dreams, down through the
a - ges the good news is heard: each of life's pag - es ex -
press - es the Word, love that en - gag - es en - flesh - es the Word.

1. Faith moves moun - tains, trans-cend-ing creeds. The
2. The poor will have priv - 'lege, the hun - gry will eat.

Word with - in words is em - bod - ied in deeds. Fear for the
All of the home - less will dance in the street. In God's rev - e -

fu - ture finds hope in the past, for love was the first word, it's
la - tion, real love will re - lease the re - in - car - na - tion of

sure - ly the last.
jus - tice and peace.

flesh - es the Word.

# HEAR GOD'S WORD

Bright as the sun, comes illumination.
When day is done, we'll walk in the light.
Hear God's Word dispel discrimination:
words of wisdom echo in the night.

> Called by God to bring Good News,
> a two-edged sword is the word we choose:
> a word of truth and integrity,
> a word to set all women free.

Relentless as rain running to the river,
a flooded plain, and nowhere to hide.
Hear God's Word, let every tyrant quiver:
all oppression will be swept aside.

> Called by God to bring Good News,
> a two-edged sword is the word we choose:
> a word of truth and integrity,
> a word to set all women free.

Strong as the tide pushing back restrictions,
when worlds collide, beware the debris.
Hear God's word proclaimed with conviction:
they move mountains who remain with Me.

> Called by God to bring Good News,
> a two-edged sword is the word we choose:
> a word of truth and integrity,
> a word to set all women free.

Fierce as a storm, terrible as thunder,
varied the form and force of Her rage.
Hear God's Word prepared to prune and plunder,
as She shapes a new and holy age.

> Called by God to bring Good News,
> a two-edged sword is the word we choose:
> a word of truth and integrity,
> a word to set all women free.

Miriam Therese Winter
Copyright © Medical Mission Sisters, 1987

# HEAR GOD'S WORD

Words and music by
Miriam Therese Winter

Bright as the sun, comes il-lu-mi-na-tion.
lent-less as rain run-ning to the riv-er, a
Strong as the tide push-ing back re-stric-tions,
Fierce as a storm, ter-ri-ble as thun-der,

When day is done, we'll walk in the light.
flood-ed plain, and no-where to hide.
when worlds col-lide, be-ware the de-bris.
var-ied the form and force of Her rage.

Hear God's Word dis-pel dis-cri-mi-na-tion:
Hear God's Word, let ev-'ry ty-rant quiv-er:
Hear God's Word pro-claimed with con-vic-tion:
Hear God's Word pre-pared to prune and plun-der,

words of wis-dom e-cho in the night.
all op-pres-sion will be swept a-side.
they move moun-tains who re-main with Me.
as She shapes a new and ho-ly age.

**Refrain**

Called by God to bring Good News, a two-edged sword is the

word we choose: a word of truth and in-teg-ri-ty, a

word to set all wom-en free.

2. Re-

# COMING AROUND AGAIN

Coming around again, it is coming around again.
A song of freedom, it is coming around again.
Look all around you, we are women and we are men,
we are singing a song of freedom,
we are coming around again.

Going and growing strong, it is going and growing strong.
The cause of justice, it is going and growing strong.
We'll build a new world in which everyone will belong.
We're promoting the cause of justice,
it is going and growing strong.

Wiping them all away, we'll be wiping them all away.
The tears of sorrow, we'll be wiping them all away.
On that day coming, we'll be practicing what we pray,
we'll be banishing tears of sorrow,
we'll be wiping them all away.

Women as well as men, we'll see women as well as men.
In all things equal, we'll see women as well as men.
The time is coming, we're not telling you where or when
we'll see all of our children equal,
we'll see women as well as men.

Coming around again, it is coming around again.
A song of freedom, it is coming around again.
Look all around you, we are women and we are men,
we are singing a song of freedom,
we are coming around, coming around,
coming around again.


Miriam Therese Winter

# COMING AROUND AGAIN

Words and music by
Miriam Therese Winter

Com - ing a - round a - gain, it is com - ing a - round a -
Go - ing and grow - ing strong, it is go - ing and grow - ing
Wip - ing them all a - way, we'll be wip - ing them all a -
Wom - en as well as men, we'll see wom - en as well as
Com - ing a - round a - gain, it is com - ing a - round a -

gain. A song of free - dom, it is com - ing a - round a -
strong. The cause of jus - tice, it is go - ing and grow - ing
way. The tears of sor - row, we'll be wip - ing them all a -
men. In all things e - qual, we'll see wom - en as well as
gain. A song of free - dom, it is com - ing a - round a -

gain. Look all a - round you, we are wom - en and we are
strong. We'll build a new world in which ev - 'ry - one will be -
way. On that day com - ing, we'll be prac - tic - ing what we
men. The time is com - ing, we're not tell - ing you where or
gain. Look all a - round you, we are wom - en and we are

_To Coda_

men, we are sing - ing a song of free - dom, we are
long. We're pro - mot - ing the cause of jus - tice, it is
pray, we'll be ban - ish - ing tears of sor - row, we'll be
when we'll see all of our chil - dren e - qual, we'll see
men, we are sing - ing a song of free - dom, we are

_Coda_

com - ing a - round a - gain. com - ing a round,
go - ing and grow - ing strong.
wip - ing them all a - way.
wom - en as well as men.

com - ing a - round, com - ing a - round a - gain.

# YOU SHALL BE MY WITNESSES

You shall be my witnesses through all the earth,
telling of all you have heard and received,
for I arose and am with you, and you have believed.

> Women at the tomb,
> weeping for the dead.
> He is not here,
> he has risen as he said.
> They ran to tell those who were in authority.
> The men dismissed the news as idle fantasy.

You shall be my witnesses through all the earth,
telling of all you have heard and received,
for I arose and am with you, and you have believed.

> Magdalene at the tomb:
> Whom do you seek?
> Her eyes were opened
> when she heard him speak.
> His love for every woman shone upon his face.
> The hopes of every age were held in their embrace.

You shall be my witnesses through all the earth,
telling of all you have heard and received,
for I arose and am with you, and you have believed.

> Women, leave your tombs.
> Roll the stones aside.
> Do not despair,
> though so many dreams have died.
> Do not be fearful of the vision that you see.
> Believe in miracles again. Believe in me.

You shall be my witnesses through all the earth,
telling of all you have heard and received,
for I arose and am with you, and you have believed.

# YOU SHALL BE MY WITNESSES

Words and music by
Miriam Therese Winter

**Refrain** ♩ = 80

You shall be my wit-ness-es through all the earth,
tell-ing of all you have heard and re-ceived, for
I a-rose and am with you and you have be-lieved.

**Verses**

Wom-en at the tomb, weep-ing for the dead:
Mag-da-lene at the tomb: Whom do you seek?
Wom-en, leave your tombs. Roll the stones a-side.

He is not here, he has ris-en as he said.
Her eyes were o-pened when she heard him speak.
Do not des-pair, though so man-y dreams have died.

They ran to tell those who were in au-thor-i-ty.
His love for ev-'ry wom-an shone up-on his face.
Do not be fear-ful of the vi-sion that you see.

The men dis-missed the news as i-dle fan-ta-sy.
The hopes of ev-'ry age were held in their em-brace.
Be-lieve in mir-a-cles a-gain. Be-lieve in me.

# COME, SPIRIT

Sing, my soul, a Spirit song,
calling all to sing along.
Fill the world with joyful sounds:
God is here and grace abounds.

Come, Spirit, come and be a new reality.
Your touch is guarantee of love alive in me.

Dance, my heart, at your rebirth,
partner to the dance of earth.
Thirsting spirit, drink your fill:
love goes dancing where it will.

Come, Spirit, come and be a new reality.
Your touch is guarantee of love alive in me.

When constrained by thoughts or things,
hear the word the Spirit brings:
life is larger than it seems,
hope is harbinger of dreams.

Come, Spirit, come and be a new reality.
Your touch is guarantee of love alive in me.

# COME, SPIRIT

Words and music by
Miriam Therese Winter

♩ = 72

C    C6    C    C6    C

Sing, my soul, a Spir - it song,
Dance, my heart, at your re - birth,
When con - strained by thoughts or things,

G7    C   G7   C    C6

call - ing all to sing a - long. Fill the world with
part - ner to the dance of earth. Thirst - ing spir - it,
hear the word the Spir - it brings: life is larg - er

C    G7    F    C

joy - ful sounds: God is here and grace a - bounds.
drink your fill: love goes danc - ing where it will.
than it seems, hope is har - bin - ger of dreams.

**Refrain**

F    G7    C

Come, Spir - it, come and be a new re - al - i - ty.

Am    Dm7    G7    F    C

Your touch is guar - an - tee of love a - live in me.

# WOMEN

Women and earth have both given birth
          to deeds that escape our detection,
but crucified reason awaited its season
          to hone its truths to perfection.
Down through the ages, wiped clean from life's pages,
          is wisdom we would bring to light,
with just retribution for each contribution
          entombed in the womb of the night,
with just retribution for each contribution
          entombed in the womb of the night.

Women in homes have written the poems
          that captured the human condition.
In public arenas, their service was seen as
          unworthy of due recognition.
Their peace and compassion, though always in fashion,
          were seldom embraced by the times.
To women belong the substance of song,
          while others have written the rhymes,
to women belong the substance of song,
          while others have written the rhymes.

Women today have something to say
        from centuries of silently waiting:
be done with the scandals of incense and candles
        to idols of your own creating.
Peace is a part of the hope at the heart of
        the carousel's clarion call,
and women are weaving a web of believing:
        their love is encompassing all,
and women are weaving a web of believing:
        their love is encompassing all.

The feminine face of the God of disgrace
        is symbol for joy and elation.
She suffered the lashes and rose from the ashes,
        transforming all degradation.
As mothers and martyrs and new movement starters,
        women have known all along:
the tears they have tasted, the gifts they have wasted,
        their love will transpose into song,
the tears they have tasted, the gifts they have wasted,
        their love will transpose into song.

Miriam Therese Winter
Copyright © Medical Mission Sisters, 1987

# WOMEN

*Words and music by
Miriam Therese Winter*

Wom - en and earth have both giv - en birth to
Wom - en in homes have writ - ten the poems that
Wom - en to - day have some - thing to say from
fe - mi - nine face of the God of dis - grace is

deeds that es - cape our de - tec - tion, but
cap - tured the hu - man con - di - tion. In
cen - turies of si - lent - ly wait - ing: be
sym - bol for joy and e - la - tion. She

cru - ci - fied rea - son a - wait - ed its sea - son to
pub - lic a - re - nas their serv - ice was seen as un -
done with the scan - dals of in - cense and can - dles to
suf - fered the lash - es and rose from the ash - es, trans -

hone its truths to per - fec - tion. Their
wor - thy of due rec - og - ni - tion.
i - dols of your own cre - a - ting.
form - ing all de - gra - da - tion. As

Down through the a - ges, wiped clean from life's pag - es, is
peace and com - pas - sion, though al - ways in fash - ion, were
Peace is a part of the hope at the heart of the
moth - ers and mar - tyrs and new move - ment start - ers,

wis - dom we would bring to light, with
sel - dom em - braced by the times. To
ca - rou - sel's cla - ri - on call, and
wom - en have known all a - long: the

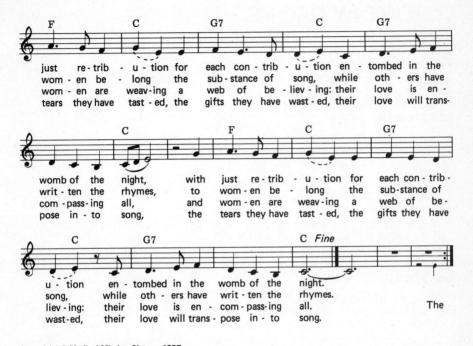

just re-trib - u - tion for each con - trib - u - tion en - tombed in the
wom - en be - long the sub-stance of song, while oth - ers have
wom - en are weav-ing a web of be - liev - ing: their love is en -
tears they have tast - ed, the gifts they have wast - ed, their love will trans-

womb of the night, with just re-trib - u - tion for each con - trib -
writ - ten the rhymes, to wom - en be - long the sub-stance of
com - pass-ing all, and wom - en are weav-ing a web of be -
pose in - to song, the tears they have tast - ed, the gifts they have

u - tion en - tombed in the womb of the night.
song, while oth - ers have writ - ten the rhymes.
liev - ing: their love is en - com-pass-ing all.
wast - ed, their love will trans - pose in - to song.

The

# A NEW DAY DAWNS

Two women care, four women dare,
and ten will follow after.
Two are few, but four are more,
and ten times ten worth waiting for.
A million strong on a single song,
soon the whole world sings along,
and a new day dawns.

> Out there on your own,
> know that you are not alone.
> Look around and see
> signs of solidarity.

Two women care, four women dare,
and ten will follow after.
Two are few, but four are more,
and ten times ten worth waiting for.
A million strong on a single song,
soon the whole world sings along,
and a new day dawns.

> When you feel harassed,
> first in line, yet always last,
> don't withdraw and hide.
> Find a friend to stand beside.

Two women care, four women dare,
and ten will follow after.
Two are few, but four are more,
and ten times ten worth waiting for.
A million strong on a single song,
soon the whole world sings along,
and a new day dawns.

> All the world at war.
> Peace eludes us more and more.
> Let us not lose heart.
> You and I can make a start.

Two women care, four women dare,
and ten will follow after.
Two are few, but four are more,
and ten times ten worth waiting for.
A million strong on a single song,
soon the whole world sings along,
and a new day dawns, and a new day dawns.

Miriam Therese Winter
Copyright © Medical Mission Sisters, 1987

# A NEW DAY DAWNS

# ONE BY ONE

One by one, we are coming to awareness.
One by one, we're committed to a cause.
One by one, we are challenging the structures.
One by one, we are changing the laws.

Side by side, we are bound to make a difference.
Side by side, that is how the spirit thrives.
Side by side, we're receiving some concessions.
Side by side, we are changing our lives.

Hand in hand, we can manage any mountain.
Hand in hand, we're accomplishing the climbs.
Hand in hand, we confront discrimination.
Hand in hand, we are changing the times.

Nationwide, we are marching on to freedom.
Nationwide, through the nights and the days.
Nationwide, we press on for liberation.
Nationwide, we are changing our ways.

Around the world, we are rising up for justice.
Around the world, they are hearing our cries.
Around the world, we are throwing off our shackles.
Around the world, we are opening our eyes.

Sisters, all, reaching out to one another.
Sisters, all, reaching up to the heights.
Sisters, all, reaching out for understanding.
Sisters, all equal, all for equal rights.

Women of the world, we're united in compassion.
Women of the world, we are one in our pain.
Women of the world, we are one in deprivation.
Women of the world, we say: Never again! Never, never again!


Miriam Therese Winter

# ONE BY ONE

Words and music by
Miriam Therese Winter

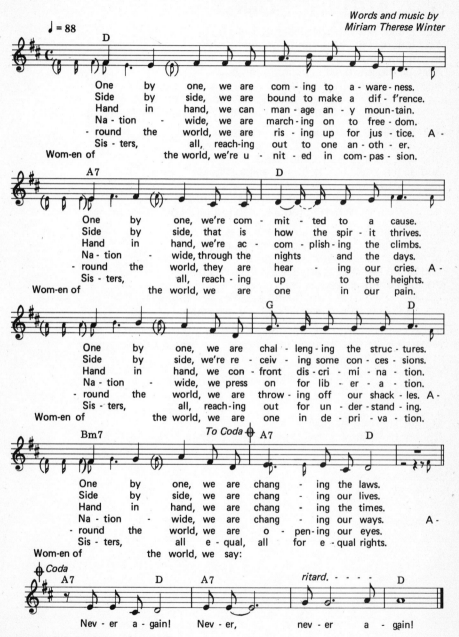

One by one, we are com-ing to a-ware-ness.
Side by side, we are bound to make a dif-f'rence.
Hand in hand, we can man-age an-y moun-tain.
Na-tion - wide, we are march-ing on to free-dom. A-
-round the world, we are ris-ing up for jus-tice. A-
Sis-ters, all, reach-ing out to one an-oth-er.
Wom-en of the world, we're u - nit-ed in com-pas-sion.

One by one, we're com-mit-ted to a cause.
Side by side, that is how the spir-it thrives.
Hand in hand, we're ac-com-plish-ing the climbs.
Na-tion - wide, through the nights and the days.
-round the world, they are hear - ing our cries. A-
Sis-ters, all, reach-ing up to the heights.
Wom-en of the world, we are one in our pain.

One by one, we are chal - leng-ing the struc-tures.
Side by side, we're re-ceiv - ing some con-ces-sions.
Hand in hand, we con-front dis-cri-mi-na-tion.
Na-tion - wide, we press on for lib-er-a-tion.
-round the world, we are throw-ing off our shack-les. A-
Sis-ters, all, reach-ing out for un-der-stand-ing.
Wom-en of the world, we are one in de-pri-va-tion.

One by one, we are chang - ing the laws.
Side by side, we are chang - ing our lives.
Hand in hand, we are chang - ing the times.
Na-tion - wide, we are chang - ing our ways. A-
-round the world, we are o - pen-ing our eyes.
Sis-ters, all e - qual, all for e - qual rights.
Wom-en of the world, we say:

Nev-er a-gain! Nev-er, nev-er a-gain!

# YOU ARE THE SONG

You spoke a word and stirred a silent spring.
You touched my heart and I began to sing,
to free the music deep in everything.
Now all the earth with its innate melody
has meaning for me forever.
>You are the song and You are the singing.
>All through the longing, You come bringing music.

You promised You would give the words to say.
You touched my heart and I began to pray,
and all my frail defenses fell away,
and all the walls that held my feelings inside
were thrown open wide forever.
>You are the prayer and You are the praying.
>When I prepare, You're there conveying music.

You promised to be present everywhere.
You touched my heart and I became aware
of all the love entrusted to my care,
and of the need to share the gift that You give,
the love that will live forever.
>You are the gift and You are the giving.
>We are uplifted, You are living...

>You are the song and You are the singing.
>All through the longing, You come bringing music.

>You are the gift and You are the giving.
>We are uplifted, You are living music.

Miriam Therese Winter
Copyright © Medical Mission Sisters, 1987

# YOU ARE THE SONG

Words and music by
Miriam Therese Winter

# TAKE THE TIME

Take the time to sing a song
for all those people who don't belong:
the women wasted by defeat,
the men condemned to walk the street,
the down and out we'll never meet.

Take the time to say a prayer
for all those people who face despair:
the starving multitudes who pray
to make it through another day,
who watch their children slip away.

Take the time to hear the plea
of every desperate refugee:
the millions who have had to flee
their lands, their loves, their liberty,
who turn in hope to you and me.

Take the time to take a stand
for peace and justice in every land.
Where power causes deep unrest,
come, take the part of the oppressed,
and then, says God, you will be blessed.


Miriam Therese Winter
Copyright © Medical Mission Sisters, 1987

# TAKE THE TIME

Words and music by
*Miriam Therese Winter*

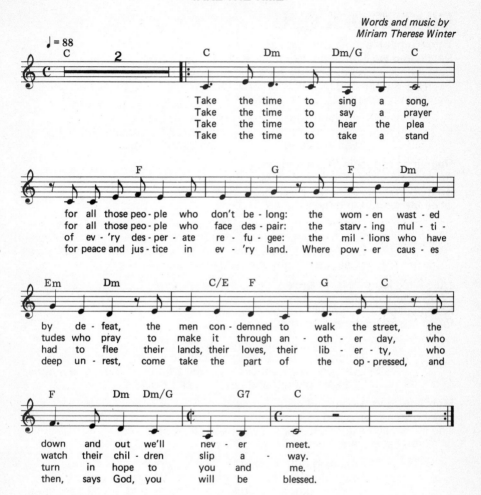

Take the time to sing a song,
for all those peo-ple who don't be-long: the wom-en wast-ed
by de-feat, the men con-demned to walk the street, the
down and out we'll nev-er meet.

Take the time to say a prayer
for all those peo-ple who face des-pair: the starv-ing mul-ti-
tudes who pray to make it through an-oth-er day, who
watch their chil-dren slip a-way.

Take the time to hear the plea
of ev-'ry des-per-ate re-fu-gee: the mil-lions who have
had to flee their lands, their loves, their lib-er-ty, who
turn in hope to you and me.

Take the time to take a stand
for peace and jus-tice in ev-'ry land. Where pow-er caus-es
deep un-rest, come take the part of the op-pressed, and
then, says God, you will be blessed.

# CIRCLE OF LOVE

Throw a pebble in a pond, see a circle.
Dance and we'll respond with a circle.
Sing a happy sound, and the song comes circling round,
'til all are caught and held in a circle of love.

> Reaching out, reaching in, a circle game: all will win.
> Teaching you, teaching me how to live inclusively.
> Everyone knows a circle grows, all around the globe it goes,
> 'til all are caught and held in a circle of love.

Rain upon a puddle falls in circles.
An echoing canyon calls in circles.
Share some happy news, it will circle back to you,
'til all are caught and held in a circle of love.

> Reaching out, reaching in, a circle game: all will win.
> Teaching you, teaching me how to live inclusively.
> Everyone knows a circle grows, all around the globe it goes,
> 'til all are caught and held in a circle of love.

Little birds learn to fly in circles.
Earth completes the sky: a circle.
Some set out to roam, yet all come circling home,
for all are caught and held in a circle of love.

> Reaching out, reaching in, a circle game: all will win.
> Teaching you, teaching me how to live inclusively.
> Everyone knows a circle grows, all around the globe it goes,
> 'til all are caught and held in a circle of love.

Marriage vows are sealed with a circle.
Rainbows are revealed as a circle.
The life we live extends through a widening circle of friends,
'til all are caught and held in a circle of love.

> Reaching out, reaching in, a circle game: all will win.
> Teaching you, teaching me how to live inclusively.
> Everyone knows a circle grows, all around the globe it goes,
> 'til all are caught and held in a circle of love.

Miriam Therese Winter
Copyright © Medical Mission Sisters, 1987

# CIRCLE OF LOVE

Words and music by
Miriam Therese Winter

♩ = 84

Throw a peb - ble in a pond, see a cir - cle.
Rain up - on a pud - dle falls in cir - cles. An
Lit - tle birds learn to fly in cir - cles.
Mar - riage vows are sealed with a cir - cle.

Dance and we'll re - spond with a cir - cle.
e - cho - ing can - yon calls in cir - cles.
Earth com - pletes the sky: a cir - cle.
Rain - bows are re - vealed as a cir - cle. The

Sing a hap - py sound, and the song comes cir - cling round, 'til
Share some hap - py news, it will cir - cle back to you, 'til
Some set out to roam, yet all come cir - cling home, for
life we live ex - tends through a widen - ing circle of friends, 'til

all are caught and held in a cir - cle of love.
all are caught and held in a cir - cle of love.
all are caught and held in a cir - cle of love.
all are caught and held in a cir - cle of love.

**Refrain**

Reach - ing out, reach - ing in, a cir - cle game: all will win.

Teach - ing you, teach - ing me, how to live in - clu - sive - ly.

Ev - 'ry - one knows a cir - cle grows, all a - round the globe it goes, 'til

all are caught and held in a cir - cle of love.

# WE ARE THE CHURCH

We are the Church.
We are a people.
We're called to bring Good News to birth.
We are the peace.
We are the promise of love outpoured
to renew the earth.

Blessed is the place of God's indwelling,
warmed by the grace embracing all.
Here God's holy Word is spoken and heard,
and people are stirred to stand together
and witness:

We are the Church.
We are a people.
We're called to bring Good News to birth.
We are the peace.
We are the promise of love outpoured
to renew the earth.

We are the place of God's indwelling,
children of grace embracing all.
The bread that we share makes us aware,
helps us prepare to praise together
and witness:

We are the Church.
We are a people.
We're called to bring Good News to birth.
We are the peace.
We are the promise of love outpoured
to renew the earth.

Miriam Therese Winter
Copyright © Medical Mission Sisters, 1987

# WE ARE THE CHURCH

Words and music by
Miriam Therese Winter

*Refrain*

We are the Church. We are a peo - ple.

We're called to bring Good News to birth. We are the peace.

We are the prom - ise of love out - poured to re - new the earth.

*Verses*

Blessed is the place of God's in - dwell - ing,
We are the place of God's in - dwell - ing,

warmed by the grace em - brac - ing all. Here God's ho - ly
chil - dren of grace em - brac - ing all. The bread that we

Word is spo - ken and heard, and peo - ple are
share makes us a - ware, helps us pre -

stirred to stand to - geth - er and wit - ness:
pare to praise to - geth - er and wit - ness:

# BLESSING SONG

May the blessing of God go before you.
May Her grace and peace abound.
May Her Spirit live within you.
May Her love wrap you 'round.
May Her blessing remain with you always.
May you walk on holy ground.


Miriam Therese Winter
Copyright © Medical Mission Sisters, 1987

# BLESSING SONG

Words and music by
Miriam Therese Winter

Sing unaccompanied
♩ = 80

(Am) May the bless - ing of God go be -

(F) fore you. May Her grace and peace a - (Am) bound. May Her

(Dm) Spir - it live with - in (Am) you. May Her (F) love (G) wrap you

(C) 'round. May Her bless - ing (F) re - main with you

(Am) al - ways. May you (Dm) walk on (Em) ho - ly (Am) ground.    Fine    D. C. al Fine

# SING OF A BLESSING

Sing, we sing of a blessing.
Sing, we sing of a blessing.
A blessing of love. A blessing of mercy.
Love will increase a blessing of peace.

Pray now, pray for a blessing.
Pray now, pray for a blessing.
A blessing of joy. A blessing of justice.
Love will increase a blessing of peace.

Share now, share in a blessing.
Share now, share in a blessing.
A blessing of hope. A blessing of courage.
Love will increase a blessing of peace.

Live, live, live as a blessing.
Live, live, live as a blessing.
A blessing within. A blessing among us.
Love will increase a blessing of peace.

Rise up, rise for a blessing.
Rise up, rise for a blessing.
A blessing be yours now and forever.
Love will increase a blessing of peace.
Love will increase a blessing of peace.

*(Alternate Final Verse)*
Send forth, send forth a blessing.
Send forth, send forth a blessing.
A blessing to all now and forever.
Love will release a blessing of peace.
Love will release a blessing of peace.


Miriam Therese Winter
Copyright © Medical Mission Sisters, 1982, 1987

## SING OF A BLESSING

Words and music by
Miriam Therese Winter

1. Sing, we sing of a bless-ing. Sing, we sing of a bless-ing.
2. Pray now, pray for a bless-ing. Pray now, pray for a bless-ing.
3. Share now, share in a bless-ing. Share now, share in a bless-ing.
*4. Live, live, live as a bless-ing. Live, live, live as a bless-ing.
**5. Rise up, rise for a bless-ing. Rise up, rise for a bless-ing.
alt. 5. Send forth, send forth a bless-ing. Send forth, send forth a bless-ing.

\* Transpose Verse 4 up one-half tone (D♭ Major).
\*\* Transpose Verse 5 up an additional half tone (D Major).

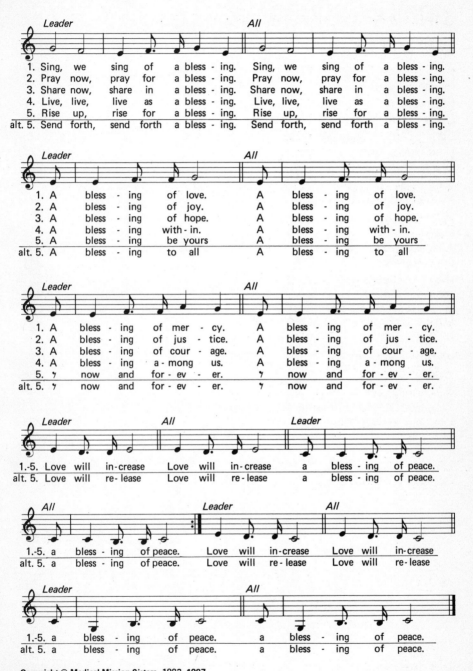

**Leader**

1. Sing, we sing of a bless - ing.
2. Pray now, pray for a bless - ing.
3. Share now, share in a bless - ing.
4. Live, live, live as a bless - ing.
5. Rise up, rise for a bless - ing.
alt. 5. Send forth, send forth a bless - ing.

**All**

Sing, we sing of a bless - ing.
Pray now, pray for a bless - ing.
Share now, share in a bless - ing.
Live, live, live as a bless - ing.
Rise up, rise for a bless - ing.
Send forth, send forth a bless - ing.

**Leader**

1. A bless - ing of love.
2. A bless - ing of joy.
3. A bless - ing of hope.
4. A bless - ing with - in.
5. A bless - ing be yours
alt. 5. A bless - ing to all

**All**

A bless - ing of love.
A bless - ing of joy.
A bless - ing of hope.
A bless - ing with - in.
A bless - ing be yours
A bless - ing to all

**Leader**

1. A bless - ing of mer - cy.
2. A bless - ing of jus - tice.
3. A bless - ing of cour - age.
4. A bless - ing a - mong us.
5. now and for - ev - er.
alt. 5. now and for - ev - er.

**All**

A bless - ing of mer - cy.
A bless - ing of jus - tice.
A bless - ing of cour - age.
A bless - ing a - mong us.
now and for - ev - er.
now and for - ev - er.

**Leader** / **All** / **Leader**

1.-5. Love will in - crease   Love will in - crease   a bless - ing of peace.
alt. 5. Love will re - lease   Love will re - lease   a bless - ing of peace.

**All** / **Leader** / **All**

1.-5. a bless - ing of peace.   Love will in - crease   Love will in - crease
alt. 5. a bless - ing of peace.   Love will re - lease   Love will re - lease

**Leader** / **All**

1.-5. a bless - ing of peace.   a bless - ing of peace.
alt. 5. a bless - ing of peace.   a bless - ing of peace.

# INDEX OF SONGS